Dear
Sebastian

Dear Sebastian

A Father's Last Wish, a Legacy of Inspiration

Compiled by Christine Horgan

HACHETTE
BOOKS
IRELAND

First published in 2009 by Hachette Books Ireland
A Hachette UK Ltd Company

ISBN 978 0 340 0 994801

Cover, text design and typesetting by Anú Design, Tara
Printed and bound in the UK by CPI Mackays, Chatham, ME5 8TD

Hachette Books Ireland policy is to use papers that are natural, renewable and recyclable
products and made from wood grown in sustainable forests. The logging and manufacturing
processes are expected to conform to the environmental regulations of the country of origin.

Hachette Books Ireland

A division _____ BH, England

For Jordan,
who has left this life for ever.

For Sebastian,
who has all his life before him.

Contents

Music, Art and Literature

Politics and State

Theatre, Television and Radio

Church, Charity and Medicine

Business, Finance and the Law

Sport

Introduction

This book is a product of deeply personal tragedy –
the worst thing that has happened to me in my life.
I lost my son, Jordan.
He died from cancer on 27 June 2008 when he was
just thirty-five years old.

It was December 2007 when Jordan, who was living in London, first began to feel unwell. He was diagnosed with influenza but, despite various treatments, the symptoms continued and became more acute as his general physical discomfort grew. Jordan continued to work, however, and, in March 2008, he went on a business trip to Sydney, Australia. While he was there, he felt extremely ill. Deeply concerned, he sought help and was admitted to St Vincent's Hospital, Sydney, where cancer was diagnosed.

After he was diagnosed, Jordan was advised by a friend, who is a psychologist, to write a final goodbye letter to Sebastian, his nine-year-old son, giving a father's advice about how best to live a happy and successful life. This was to be his last paternal gift. While considering his letter, Jordan decided to ask many notable Irish people, from various walks of life, to write similar letters, which could be compiled into a book for Sebastian to keep.

He wished to give something special to Sebastian to cherish all his life. He also hoped that it would be of benefit to other children facing the loss of a parent.

Jordan had begun this book as a diary, starting with his journey to Australia. His health deteriorated very quickly, however, and I have finished the story to the best of my ability with just the bare facts about the events leading up to his death.

I have not tried to describe in detail my feelings during this time for two reasons: it would be too painful for me and it would not be in keeping with the character of the book of letters that Jordan wanted. Those who have contributed come from all walks of life: the arts, religion, business, sport and politics. Many have shared very personal and sad stories but, in spite of setbacks, they have all achieved success by putting their various talents to best purpose. I hope that Sebastian will gain comfort and inspiration from them.

Jordan was, even as a small child, independent. He had a free and creative spirit which showed itself in his love of travelling. He was a determined person, resolute in achieving success in any projects he set himself, but he was also compassionate and sensitive with a generous nature – often to the point of extravagance! He lived for the moment, and was positive and optimistic until the day he died. This is meant to be a positive book.

Sadly, the work was only in the initial stages when Jordan died very suddenly – and without having written his own letter. I gave him my word of honour that I would finish the book if he did not have the time to, and I now have fulfilled my promise.

This is Sebastian's legacy from his father.

The week that everything changed

Jordan wrote the first part of this chapter. It is the story of the days before he was diagnosed. It is unfinished.

I try to piece together the events that happened in the second part and the chapter concludes with a letter from Clodagh Ross-Hamid, a great friend of Jordan's from his childhood days in Kinsale, who lives outside Sydney. She visited him on the day he was diagnosed and tells of his response to the frightening realisation that, at the age of thirty-four, he was terminally ill.

10 March 2008

The Oriental in Bangkok has always been my favourite hotel in the world. While there are more luxurious five stars in existence, the Oriental, on the banks of the Chao Phraya River, has a unique, old-world glamour. My being at this hotel normally means one of two things: either I am passing through Bangkok en route to a business meeting or I am on holiday with my son, Sebastian. Business trips tend to entail wild nights in a myriad of different drinking dens along Sukhumvit Road and elsewhere. City tourist boards the world over may overuse the phrase, but Bangkok truly is a city that never sleeps. It's only when the garish neon lights fade and the immaculately turned out Bangkok school children begin to appear that I know it's time to make it back to the relative sanctuary of the Oriental.

Trips with Sebastian are different, but better. His fascination with the city is contagious. He loves to spend his savings in the outdoor markets of Patpong. Sebastian, along with the thousands of other tourists, pores over the watches, computer games and ornaments in the early evening heat, while I try to distract his curious gaze from the strip bars that line these famous streets. Sebastian hasn't quite mastered the art of bargaining yet, so we tend to perform as a duo, with me baulking at the requested prices. He likes to chat about the successful negotiations and low prices we achieved while we make our way back to the Oriental by taxi (my preference) or tuk tuk (Sebastian's preference, despite the fumes, heat and dubious driving).

This trip to Bangkok is very different, though, as I am here to recuperate. I am on my way to Sydney from London for work, but have decided to stop for a weekend in Bangkok to see if I can shake off my two-month-old flu. My doctor has assured me that 'if it's a virus, the warm weather will clear it up'. My two days are spent lazing by the pool, soaking up the hot Thai sun, nibbling on keng massaman and other nutritious local dishes – and wondering if my heavy fatigue is a result of jet lag or my ongoing illness. A pretty American girl smiles at me from her lounger opposite and repeatedly follows me into the pool. Normally, this sort of thing has a fairly predictable and pleasurable outcome, but, this time, I simply leave the pool or roll over on my lounger. This can't be jet lag – I really must be sick. Evenings are spent enjoying Thai massage. I have given up on the most luxurious of Bangkok's spas, like the Banyan Tree, and reverted to the more authentic low-key Thai massage parlours, where ten or more clients, separated only by thin curtains, lie on mats in one open room. I practise my Thai with the chatty masseuses from Isaan (Thailand's northeastern region), who giggle and chat in equal measure. When our banter moves on to discuss family, it makes me wish that Sebastian was here, lying on the next mat. He is ticklish and often breaks into loud uncontrollable laughter, much to the annoyance of other weary customers and the amusement of the masseuses.

11 March 2008

The Sydney Marriott Hyde Park is basic but pleasant. I have chosen this hotel because it fits my company's budget (although very well funded, we are a start-up and it's inappropriate to luxuriate in Orientalesque establishments) and because of its location, a stone's throw from our Australian partners, who are in the American Express building on the other side of the park.

I am currently the European managing director at a company called Videoegg. We like to think of ourselves as a smart bunch of internet entrepreneurs and, although we are not changing the world (online video advertising within social networks), it feels good to be breaking new ground and creatively helping a start-up company to grow. We have managed to raise many millions from well-known investors and are confident that we can succeed in building a huge company, making ourselves wealthy and our investors wealthier. The other principals of the company work in San Francisco, while I look after international expansion from London.

Rob, Nik, Ruud, Anthony (our Australian partners) and I sit down to lunch at an outdoor restaurant in Hyde Park. They are a good bunch and we are pleased to see each other. After some preliminary personal chat, we talk excitedly about our plans and prospects in Australia. Owing to my lost luggage, I look like a tourist among business people, but I am quietly happy to be wearing a T-shirt in the warm Sydney weather. Although our conversation is punctuated by my incessant coughing, we cover quite a bit of ground and talk about the next day's conference at which we are exhibiting. Following lunch, I decide to nip to a chemist for more medication. After a short conversation with a pharmacist, I decide to go to a nearby walk-in doctor's clinic. This leads to a long wait, a series of questions about my symptoms and a blood test. This is an almost identical sequence of events to the two doctors I have recently visited in London. This doctor thinks I have glandular fever, but he tosses me an HIV leaflet to read in advance of the following day's results. I mentally check off each symptom before leaving the surgery in a state of terror.

These were the last words Jordan wrote for this book. I must now, from details sent to me from Australia by Clodagh and his colleagues, try to piece together the sequence of events that unfolded. It is most distressing for me, and I cannot write with Jordan's eloquence, but I shall try to explain what happened.

During the next few days, while waiting for the results of the blood test, Jordan attended the exhibition called AdTech in the Hilton Hotel and planned to rest at his own hotel over the weekend. He talked to his business partners about feeling unwell and the possibility that he might have glandular fever.

On Saturday, 15 March, however, he received the results from the blood tests, and they indicated the possibility of some form of cancer. He was admitted to St Vincent's Hospital for further tests. He also had a strange lump on his shoulder.

It was only at this stage that Jordan phoned me in the middle of the night (Irish time) to tell me what was happening. I cannot describe the sinking feeling in the pit of my stomach as he told me the dreadful news. Through many phone calls and emails to his Blackberry, we both clung to the thought that it was glandular fever or, at worst, that he had a lymphoma, both of which meant that his illness was curable. For several days, we both spent a lot of time checking the internet for answers and questioning any medics we knew about the implications of these two possible outcomes.

Everyone in Australia was incredibly supportive. Clodagh emailed and phoned Jordan constantly. His friends from Videoegg visited him every day, taking him DVDs to watch. They felt that he was 'definitely staying strong, although his voice was a little different'. He also emailed me to say that his ex-wife, Teena, who was in England with Sebastian, 'had been absolutely amazing'. I felt totally inadequate being so far away. Videoegg offered to pay for me to travel to Sydney, but Jordan, with his usual independence, insisted that I waited awhile because he would probably be home for treatment very soon. Little did I know how prophetic these words would be.

On the next Wednesday, 19 March, the Australian doctors decided to do a biopsy on the lump on his shoulder. I think at this stage they had already discovered a number of tumours in his body. Although Jordan told others that he was fairly confident that the now-probable diagnosis of lymphoma would be highly treatable, he emailed me otherwise. 'I am trying to think positively but I get waves of being uncontrollably petrified (in which case I ask for sleeping tablets) but there's nothing to do other than wait for a diagnosis now.'

Holy Thursday, 20 March 2008 was the day all our lives changed for ever. The diagnosis of terminal cancer was so devastating that I could hardly comprehend it. While the primary cancer had been very small, it had spread aggressively. I have no recollection now of what we said to each other. Jordan told me that the doctors had said he must fly home the next day or else 'he wouldn't make it' – this reality was incomprehensible. In my panic, I think I probably just talked about the details of what flight he would get back to England and that I would be at Heathrow airport to meet him.

Later that day, he phoned Clodagh. I shall be ever grateful to her for 'being there' for him on what must have been the darkest day of his life. I will now share with you the story of that day as she wrote it to me.

Dear Christine,

In response to your letter regarding the details of Jordan's time in Sydney, I will outline my memory of the 20 March to you.

Jordan phoned me at 4 p.m. His voice was very shaky and he talked very quickly, asking me to come to the hospital straight away. I asked him to slow down and tell me what had happened. He then told me that eight doctors had just left his room, having told him that he had a cancer so extensive that there was no hope for successful treatment and that the prognosis was very poor. I told him I would be there immediately. I dropped everything at home, left my children there, and caught a train to the city. Unfortunately, I live about twenty-five miles from Sydney and it took about an hour and a half for me to get to the hospital. I was absolutely disoriented with fear at what Jordan had told me. When I arrived, he was waiting outside the hospital. It was a dark and warm evening and he looked almost his usual self in cargo pants and a Lacoste polo shirt. The only giveaway was the padding on his neck from the biopsy. We walked to a park across the road and sat under a tree and underneath a huge depiction of the Menorah candles painted on the side of the Sydney Jewish Museum next door.

We were both crying. Jordan told me that when he saw such a delegation of doctors coming through the ward door, he knew the news would not be good, but that he never thought for a second that they were coming to tell him his life was coming to an end. They spent about an hour with him and all through that time, they tried to reiterate the extent of the cancer, while Jordan tried to talk about treatments. From what I understand, they gave him no hope at all, with a prognosis of six weeks to three months without treatment and the possibility of nine months with palliative chemotherapy. They were obviously aware of Jordan's status as a visitor to Sydney and I think they were careful about what they said, as they knew Jordan would go through all this again in Ireland. As far as I remember, they recommended no treatment other than pain relief for his symptoms because they thought he would have a better quality of life.

After the doctors left, I think they sent in the hospital social worker (Rose or Rosalie – I spoke to her once about Jordan's belongings) and they also sent for the Irish chaplain in Sydney, Fr Tom Devereux, but I am not sure if Jordan met him or not. Jordan was given anti-anxiety medication by a nurse he was friendly with. When he jokingly asked if he could have some more, she told him that because his status had changed to terminally ill, they would restrict the sleep and anti-anxiety medications they had been giving to him since he was admitted, in a bid to prevent any suicidal behaviour. Jordan saw some black humour in this and in the horror of the situation, sitting under the tree, we actually laughed about it.

Jordan immediately began talking about Sebastian and yourself. Both of you were his predominant concerns – though his feelings were different towards each of you. Where Sebastian was concerned, he talked about how he believed that Sebastian would ultimately be OK; he was young and resilient, and how he was glad that Teena had a relationship with a man whom he felt would be a good father-figure to Sebastian. We talked about the day Sebastian was born, about how helpless he had felt after Teena had given birth, how he had known it was time for him to take on the mantle of being a parent, and how overwhelmed he had been by all that that entailed. He remembered being horrified by the blood on the floor that no one came to clean up, and the desolation and loneliness he had felt in that London hospital where Sebastian was born, of his feeling that events were being taken outside his control. He talked about his feelings of failure and the sense of aloneness when his marriage had ended in Singapore, and how hard it was to lose his little family and start life again as a single man. He also spoke of his own father passing away in a car crash when he *was nine years old, and how he felt that Sebastian's youth would help him to cope with Jordan's death. He broke down again when he said that he didn't know how he was going to tell Sebastian that his father was going to die.*

I think he had already spoken with you and Teena before I had arrived at the hospital and I was worried about you because I know that a phone call like that from twelve thousand miles away must have been agonising, so I asked Jordan if I could call you later that night. He agreed and asked me to stay in touch with you after his funeral as you did not really know his work colleagues and he was very anxious that you would have someone to talk with about him. At that point, I was trying to deflect any talk of dying and funerals, but he was adamant. Although he was obviously under the influence of anti-anxiety pills, he was very clear-headed and precise about what he wanted. He told me that he expected that you would have a brave face throughout the grieving process, but that, inside and at home, you would crumble. And he was desperately worried about that. He told me that you had absolutely adored him all his life and he told me how much he loved you.

Jordan had been very happy with the level of care he had received at St Vincent's and I think he would have considered staying for treatment if they had given him any hope at all. When he realised that this was not the case, he was anxious to get to you as soon as possible. He wanted to stay until the following Tuesday after Easter to travel, but the doctors told him that they could not guarantee that he would be in any condition to travel by then, and they recommended that he leave as soon as possible. Jordan called his airline to change his flight plans, and when he asked for an upgrade from Economy to Business Class, he was told flatly by the telephone operator that 'This airline does not give upgrades on the basis of a terminally ill passenger' and we had a bit of a joke about what someone had to do to get an upgrade from an airline. That was another thing that Jordan found blackly funny, especially when the operator went on to ask if he would still like his pre-booked, three-day stopover in Bangkok. 'Under the given circumstances,' Jordan told her, 'I think not.' Later, he told me that maybe he should have taken the stopover in Thailand as one last hurrah!

He went on to talk about how he had been so grateful for the life he had led, for the travel he had done and everything he had seen. And even though he would probably be dead at thirty-five, he was so happy that he had led his life the way he had. That he would have preferred it to working in an office all his life and living until he was eighty. He told me, though, that he had never once considered the possibility that something like this could happen, and had always thought that if he were to pass away early, it would be through a plane or car crash. He thought this was more likely, given the kind of life he led.

He was very concerned about his financial situation and about the financial legacy he would leave Sebastian. He had already telephoned his company's head office to check whether he had a death benefit policy, with Sebastian listed as the main benefactor. He was very anxious that he should not leave you with any financial and administrative entanglements to have to sort out after his death.

He talked about male friends he had in the UK who were still living as bachelors without children and how he was so thankful that he was leaving a son behind him. Sebastian was his most proud achievement, I think, in the final analysis. He was confident about a bright future for his son, but was very worried about how he was going to prepare Sebastian for his death.

Jordan knew that he would have to undertake the whole testing process again when he returned to Ireland, and told me of his aversion to the injections and the treatment. He said that, in a way, the diagnosis was a vague relief, as he was beginning to feel that some of the doctors had thought his symptoms were psychosomatic. I asked him how he felt physically, and he said that he could feel the cancer everywhere, *and could feel it actively moving as we sat there, and how he woke up nearly every morning with a new symptom. We talked about why it hadn't been picked up earlier in England and he told me about the timeline of events there – that he had been feeling unwell by the end of 2007 and, in February, they had told him it was a bad dose of the flu and had sent him for blood tests based on the possibility of a blood disorder or an exotic disease like malaria (owing to his extensive travels), but how the doctors never once mentioned the possibility of cancer.*

Initially, when I saw him, he had told me that he didn't want to speak to anyone else that evening apart from yourself and Teena, but after we had talked, he said that it felt cathartic and that he would call a couple of his close friends in the UK. He was very tired, and I was anxious that he should get a good night's sleep to help prepare him for his journey the following day, so I walked him back to the hospital.

It was very hard, and, Christine, I am telling you these things in a matter-of-fact way, which is very different to how I feel inside, but I understand my place in this whole situation. Although I am devastated at the loss of my beautiful friend of twenty years, Jordan's death is not my own personal tragedy – it is yours, and Sebastian's, and Jordan's, and I have no right to burden you with my sadness and grief.

We said our goodbyes to one another and formally thanked each other for the friendship and support for one another since 1988. We spoke of our love and appreciation for each other. I think this was Jordan's first farewell to life, his first goodbye to a friend and it was very shocking. I gave him two home-made 'Get Well' cards that my children had made for him and he called me back to the door of the hospital and said, 'Whatever happens in your life, always take care of your children.' Those were his last words to me. I came straight home and telephoned you.

Clodagh

The last three months at home

As I stood at the arrivals gate of Terminal 4 in Heathrow airport, my mind was in turmoil. Waiting seemed to take for ever and, as it turned out, Jordan was last through Customs because the airline had lost his suitcase. As I waited, more and more dramatic scenarios went through my head. Had he been taken so ill that he'd been driven off in an ambulance unbeknownst to me? Had he never made it to the plane and was dying alone in Australia? A man standing beside me cheerily said, 'Isn't it marvellous to see everyone so happy coming home?' I attempted a weak smile.

Finally my beloved son was with me and we travelled back to his apartment where we both cried and promised each other that we would face the future together and fight this dreadful affliction to the best of our ability. It was Easter weekend and so my husband, Pat (Jordan's stepfather), had made an appointment for him with an oncologist in Cork for the following Tuesday. After a frightening two days in London, in which Jordan was in continuous pain, we flew back to Cork on Easter Monday. By then, he could hardly walk and was in such agony that Pat drove him to the Mercy Hospital the second we arrived. Within one hour, the oncologist (whom Jordan later described as 'direct yet compassionate') came in, in his weekend jeans, and gave us the news that the average lifetime expectancy at this stage for this type of cancer was four to six months. We were shattered. I had no idea that Jordan had already been given a shorter time than this by the doctors in Sydney.

He stayed in hospital for a few days while they alleviated the pain and then came home to Kinsale to face whatever lay ahead. This became a nightmare of up to thirty tablets over each twenty-four-hour period and a daily injection because of a blood clot that had developed in his leg. Jordan had chemotherapy which, he said, 'wiped him out'. The pain reoccurred intermittently in different parts of his body and with varying severity. He tried short spells on different diets and drank a copious amount of fruit and vegetable juices and smoothies. Sleeping became difficult and in an email to a friend he wrote, 'I find it hard to switch off at night. I don't tend to dwell on why any longer, but I find it hard to daydream in the way I used to before sleep. So much of my night-time thoughts used to be about the future which is less applicable these days!'

Most of his worries were about Sebastian, and this is how the idea of this book came about. Jordan was shattered at the thought that he would not be around to give Sebastian his love and guidance as he grew up.

During Jordan's illness, Sebastian came to visit from England several times with his mother, Teena, and some of Jordan's friends flew in from England to see him too. Jordan, Sebastian, Pat and I had one lovely week together in a holiday village, go-karting, playing crazy golf and generally having a fun time.

By the week of 6 June, everything looked a little brighter. Several replies had arrived to the trial letters which we had been sent out looking for contributions to *Dear Sebastian*, the title he had decided upon for the book. Jordan had been interviewed on *Today with Pat Kenny* and had met Gráinne McBride, who was writing a piece about him and the planned book in the *Irish Examiner*. More importantly still, the tumours had shrunk as a result of chemotherapy and the oncologist gave him a three-month respite to travel before his next appointment. But it was not to be.

The next weekend, 14 June, Jordan travelled up to Dublin by

train and flew to Zurich to go to the Italy versus Romania Euro 2008 group match with a friend. I had hastily learned to text in order to keep in touch and to remind Jordan of the times when he had to take his tablets. He sounded to be in good form. However, when he arrived back on the Sunday night, he was in severe pain. For the next few days, his medication was increased and changed many times, but without much success. On Friday, 20 June, he was admitted to Marymount Hospice in Cork, so that his condition could be monitored. They assured me that he would probably be home by the following Tuesday.

Sunday, 22 June is a day I shall never forget. I was told the devastating news by the medical staff that Jordan probably had less than a week to live. There was nothing else they could do. I was allowed to stay by his side night and day. Sebastian and Teena came, as did Aki, one of his great friends who travelled from Dubai. His stepsisters, Elaine, Colette and Clara, were there too. Much of the time, he was only semiconscious from the painkillers, but I tried to keep everything as normal as possible. He could hear life going on in the ward and I gave him up-to-date news on all the football matches. Typically, at one point, he told me to go home, but I assured him that I intended staying until we could go out of the hospice together. I prayed that he did not realise that we would go out through different doors.

At 7.05 a.m. on Friday, 27 June 2008, Jordan died peacefully with me by his side. I kept repeating how much I loved him. He was buried on 1 July and many, many, of his wonderful friends came from all round the world to accompany him on his last journey. I had promised him that I would finish his book if he did not have the time to, and, apart from cherishing and loving Sebastian, this is the last thing I can do for my darling son.

A note to Sebastian

I want to tell you about the wonderful book your dad has left for you. Your dad loved you greatly and wished to leave you something that would be a lifelong gift. Your future was so important to him – he wanted you to be happy and successful and was grief-stricken that he would not be around to help you throughout your life. Even though he was feeling so sick, he had the determination and courage to go ahead with this project. It is sad that he didn't have time to write his own letter to you. I have tried to give you a few ideas about what he might have said in my own letter, which is at the end of this book.

I also feel that it is important for me to tell you that all the generous Irish people who have contributed to this book have done so purely out of compassion and sympathy for you and your situation. I have met only three of them, one of whom wishes to remain anonymous, and had never had any contact with the others before the initial letter asking them to take part in the project. None of them was aware that a portion of the proceeds from the book would go to the Irish Hospice Foundation.

Throughout the book, you will find some words in the Irish language and reference to various Irish institutions. As you have always lived in England, these may not be familiar to you, so I have added a glossary of terms which I hope will help you understand more clearly what has been written.

Grandma Ireland
Kinsale, County Cork, April 2009

Glossary

APGAI
Association of Professional Game Angling Instructors

Beir bua agus beannacht
Good luck and blessings

Ceann Comhairle
Speaker/Chairperson (sole judge of order in Dáil Éireann)

CIÉ (Córas Iompair Éireann)
Irish public bus and rail transport authority

Dáil Éireann
The Irish House of Representatives (lower House of Parliament)

Dia leat
Bless you

ESB
Electricity Supply Board

Fáilte Ireland
National Tourist Development Authority

FÁS (Foras Áiscanna Saothair)
National Training and Employment Authority

Fianna Fáil
Irish republican political party (in power at time of writing in 2008)

Fine Gael
Irish political party (in opposition at time of writing in 2009)

Flaithiúleach
(Slang) Generous

GAA (Gaelic Athletic Association)
Promotes traditional Irish sports, e.g. Gaelic football, hurling, etc.

Go n-éirí leat
Wishing you success

IBEC
Irish Business and Employers Confederation

Is mise le meas
Yours sincerely

Le grá go deo
With love for ever

Oireachtas
Parliament of Ireland. Consists of the President, Dáil Éireann
and Seanad Éireann

RTÉ (Raidio Teilifís Éireann)
National television and radio station

Seanad Éireann
The Senate (upper House of Parliament)

Tanaiste
Deputy Irish Prime Minister

Taoiseach
Irish Prime Minister

TD (Teachta Dála)
Deputy to the Dáil (member of parliament)

Telecom Éireann
The Irish Telecommunications Board

vas writing a lot of tiresome old waffle that might make m
k great but would not be much good to you. Writing the le
made me realise something a bit humbling for a paren
n no expert. My wife and I have three sons, all grown u
v, decent generous, funny human beings. We are very prou
them but that's the way parents are. The truth is th
ey turned out well because of the decisions they made. Ye
ey always knew they were loved, as you are, and they did n
ve to worry about having a comfortable nest in which
e, but they still had important decisions to make. You w
cide what kind of person you will be. A parent can hope a

Letters to the
Contributors

courage, but the decision is yourself. You will ultimately ta
e credit for the person that you will become,
cide now on some of your choices. Kind or cruel? Genero
mean? Honourable and honest or crooked and sleazy? A lo
ne ago, on a fishing trip with my late, great, dear friend, v
re chatting after dinner and, in the way adults do after
ple of glasses of wine, I posed the philosophical questio
hat's it all about?' To my surprise, he didn't hesitat
at's easy. It's about doing the right thing.' Then, not f
e first time in my life, I deployed my mouth without actua
engaging my brain. I asked, 'How do you know what th
nt thing is?' His answer was irrefutable. 'That's the poin
u always know what the right thing is.' It's true, and if ye
nt the simple, waffle-free philosophy to guide your lif
at's it. The 'right thing' is not always the easiest of mo
nvenient thing, but you will know what it is, even when
es against the common consensus, perhaps the views of yo
ends. You will know what's right. Your life; your choice. I-
ay to make mistakes from time to time, so long as you lea
m them. Don't hold grudges. Don't expect anyone else to l
-fect. By now, your mum and dad will have set your mor
npass and you will know right from wrong. The rest is up
a. Have a good life, Sebastian. Do the right thing. I aske
w do you know what the right thing is?' His answer w
efutable. 'That's the point. You always know what the rig

1 May 2008

Dear _____

I am writing to you to ask for a short submission for inclusion in the upcoming publication *Dear Sebastian. Dear Sebastian* is a collection of short letters of advice from the most accomplished Irish leaders within business, sport, the world of art, literature, entertainment, politics and religion.

The background to this project is that at the age of thirty-four I have recently been diagnosed with terminal cancer. Prior to this I was healthy and fit and enjoyed working in London as a Managing Director of a successful Internet company. I am now at home in Ireland focusing full-time on fighting cancer through chemotherapy and other methods, in an effort to maximise the quality and quantity of my life.

At my doctor's suggestion, I am preparing to write a goodbye letter to my nine-year-old son Sebastian, in which I will offer my thoughts and advice on how to live a happy and full life. In conjunction with this, I have decided to set about compiling *Dear Sebastian*, which will be published in 2009.

I am sure that you are extremely busy but I know that Sebastian and the readers of *Dear Sebastian* would be very interested to learn what you consider to be the most important guidelines in order to live a happy and fulfilled life. Ideally your letter to Sebastian would include pieces of advice, illustrated with examples from your real life experiences as a _____, and elsewhere, if possible.

I do hope that you will participate in this unique project. If you have any questions or comments regarding *Dear Sebastian*, please don't hesitate to contact me for further information.

Yours sincerely

Jordan M. Ferguson

11 August 2008

Dear _____

Last Easter, my son Jordan Ferguson, then aged thirty-four, was diagnosed with terminal cancer. He took this news with great fortitude and courage and his only concern was for his nine-year-old son Sebastian.

Whilst having treatment and trying to fight this disease he was encouraged to write a goodbye letter to him with his thoughts and advice about how to live a happy and fulfilled life. This led to the idea for the book *Dear Sebastian*, which Jordan intended to be a compilation of similar letters from the most accomplished Irish leaders within business, design, entertainment, politics, religion and sport.

Sadly, Jordan died much earlier than we all expected on 27 June. He had only written a few letters to prospective contributors, many of whom have generously responded already. As devastated as I am, I must now finish the project as a legacy to young Sebastian and in memory of Jordan. I am therefore respectfully asking you to write a letter to Sebastian with what you consider to be the most important guidelines to give him. Jordan was hoping that you would include a small personal anecdote which might have led you to certain beliefs in life. I am enclosing an article all about the book which *The Irish Examiner* published after hearing Jordan on the radio show *Today with Pat Kenny*.

I am sure that you are extremely busy but would be most grateful if you would participate in this unique project.

Do please contact me if you need any further information.

Yours sincerely

Christine J. Horgan

The Letters

vas writing a lot of tiresome old waffle that might make r
k great but would not be much good to you. Writing the le
- made me realise something a bit humbling for a paren
n no expert. My wife and I have three sons, all grown
w, decent generous, funny human beings. We are very pro
them but that's the way parents are. The truth is th
ey turned out well because of the decisions they made. Ye
ey always knew they were loved, as you are, and they did n
ve to worry about having a comfortable nest in which
e, but they still had important decisions to make. You v
cide what kind of person you will be. A parent can hope a
courage, but the decision is yours. You will ultimately ta
e credit, or the blame, for the person you will become,
cide now on some of your choices. Kind or cruel? Genero
mean? Honourable and honest or crooked and sleazy? A lo
ne ago, on a fishing trip with a gentle, generous friend, v
re chatting after dinner and, in the way adults do after
aple of glasses of wine, I posed the philosophical questio
'hat's it all about?' To my surprise, he didn't hesita
nat's easy. It's about doing the right thing.' Then, not f
e first time in my life, I deployed my mouth without actu
engaging my brain. I asked, 'How do you know what t
ht thing is?' His answer was irrefutable. 'That's the poin
u always know what the right thing is.' It's true, and if y
nt the simple, waffle-free philosophy to guide your lif
at's it. The 'right thing' is not always the easiest or mc
nvenient thing, but you will know what it is, even when
es against the common consensus, perhaps the views of yc
ends. You will know what's right. Your life; your choice. I
ay to make mistakes from time to time, so long as you lea
om them. Don't hold grudges. Don't expect anyone else to
rfect. By now, your mum and dad will have set your mo
mpass and you will know right from wrong. The rest is up
u. Have a good life, Sebastian. Do the right thing. I aske
ow do you know what the right thing is?' His answer w
efutable. 'That's the point. You always know what the rig

was writing a lot of tiresome old waffle that might make
k great but would not be much good to you. Writing the le
made me realise something a bit humbling for a paren
m no expert. My wife and I have three sons, all grown
w, decent generous, funny human beings. We are very pro
them but that's the way parents are. The truth is th
ey turned out well because of the decisions they made. Ye
ey always knew they were loved, as you are, and they did
ve to worry about having a comfortable nest in which
e, but they still had important decisions to make. You
cide what kind of person you will be. A parent can hope a

Music, Art

courage, but the decision is yours. You will ultimately ta
e credit, or the for the man you will become,
cide now on some of your choices. Kind or cruel? Genero

and Literature

mean? Honourable and honest or crooked and sleazy? A lo
ne ago, on a fishing trip with a good friend, w
re chatting after dinner and, in the way adults do after
ple of glasses of wine, I posed the philosophical questio
hat's it all about?' To my surprise, he didn't hesita
at's easy. It's about doing the right thing.' Then, not f
e first time in my life, I deployed my mouth without actu
engaging my brain. I asked, 'How do you know what t
ht thing is?' His answer was irrefutable. 'That's the poi
u always know what the right thing is.' It's true, and if y
nt the simple, waffle-free philosophy to guide your li
at's it. The 'right thing' is not always the easiest of mo
nvenient thing, but you will know what it is, even when
es against the common consensus, perhaps the views of yo
ends. You will know what's right. Your life; your choice. I
ay to make mistakes from time to time, so long as you lea
om them. Don't hold grudges. Don't expect anyone else to
rfect. By now, your mum and dad will have set your mo
mpass and you will know right from wrong. The rest is up
u. Have a good life, Sebastian. Do the right thing. I aske
ow do you know what the right thing is?' His answer w
efutable. 'That's the point. You always know what the rig

8 September 2008

Dear Sebastian,

My name is Christy Moore. I am a singer.
You and I have something in common. I lost
my dad when I was 11. I will never forget
that day, the way I felt, the things that
happened.

I heard about your dad's idea for letters.
He had so much love for you to set this idea
in motion.

I loved my father. I have held on to that
love for many years now. Often at night,
when it is dark and quiet, I remember him
and the love we had. I ask him for guidance
when I have a problem. I believe he
watches over me and is my guiding light.

I am much older now but I still remember
him clearly. Even this morning, as I write
these few lines, I feel him close to me. I am
looking at the photo of you and your dad on
the beach with his arm upon your shoulder.

The love that is there, will always be with you.

Today, I am going to the studio to record some songs.

I will sing one for you.

Sincerely,

Christy Moore

Christy Moore

Christy Moore is a popular folk singer-songwriter whose songs often reflect social commentary. He was voted Ireland's Greatest Living Musician in 2007.

Dear Sebastian,

I've been thinking about what I should say to you for a while. To give someone advice on how best to live their life is a big ask.

For myself, I have always tried to do what I thought was right. You will soon go to secondary school and I think it's important that you don't just follow what everyone else does. It takes a strong character to stand back from the crowd and be an individual.

You will or you may have already discovered talents that you have or find things that you can do that will fill you with enthusiasm. Whatever these might be, try to pursue them and give them your all.

As your life progresses, be grateful for whatever success you might achieve, but never forget that no man is an island and that without friends and loved ones, success is of little value.

Above all, Sebastian, remember that although your father was taken from you, as mine was, at an early age, it is my belief that remembering the love and concern he had for you will help you if at any time life is difficult.

I wish you all the best. Maybe we will meet one day.

God bless

Daniel O'Donnell

Daniel O'Donnell

Daniel O'Donnell is one of Ireland's best-loved singers of country, folk and easy-listening songs. He has recorded 39 albums, selling over 10 million copies and performs to over 500,000 people every year from Carnegie Hall to the Sydney Opera House. He has won many awards including numerous music awards, a Lifetime Achievement Award from the *Irish Post* in London, an honorary MBE for services to the music industry and charity, and the Michael Aspel *This is Your Life* tribute.

From: Nell McCafferty

To: Christine Horgan

Sent: 10 October 2008 01:09

Subject: Dear Sebastian

Dear Sebastian,

Your father loved you. He said so, wrote so and told the world about how he loved his son.

I am glad that you will always know that. A father's love is a blessing.

Nell

Nell McCafferty

Born in Derry, Nell McCafferty spent her early career as a journalist commenting on events in Northern Ireland. She is outspoken on her views on feminism, abortion, contraception and euthanasia and she has also become well-known as a civil rights campaigner. In 1990, she won a Jacob's Award for her reports for RTÉ Radio on the World Cup football finals.

Dear Sebastian,

This must be the hardest letter I've ever had to write in my life. On reading your grandmother's letter to me asking me to contribute to your late dad's idea for you, I was speechless. He sounds like he was a very brave, loving and proud dad. Having recently become a dad myself, your dad's story really struck a nerve with me. It's heartbreaking. However, he started something for you, Sebastian, and here's my little part in this amazing idea he had for you.

Sebastian, I've never really been one to give advice but one thing my parents always taught me is that nobody is better than you and you're better than nobody. As people we are all equal. Some may have more money, some may have less, but, above all that, we are all equal.

Something, I will always try to instil into my 2 young boys, Rocco and Jay, is to have a goal or goals in life and to go for them!

Live the dream! Because you never know, Sebastian, dreams sometimes do come true!

By the way, as a dad, I know that your dad loved you with all his heart. Go on make him proud...!

Le grá go deo!

Nicky Byrne 2008.

Nicky Byrne

Born in Dublin, Nicky Byrne joined the Sligo-based band Westlife in 1998. Before starting his singing career, he had a career in football and was a member of several clubs, including Home Farm and Leeds Utd, as well as playing with the Irish youth national football teams.

Dear Sebastian,

My name is Joseph O'Connor and I am 45, which I imagine must seem quite old to you, as it sometimes does to me. When I was the age you are now, my own father turned 30, and I can clearly remember thinking to myself that it seemed an absolutely ancient age, like a dinosaur's, and it was unimaginable to me that, one day, I, myself, would be 30, never mind a staggering 45. In fact, just writing that now, I find myself remembering that feeling.

I'm writing to you, Sebastian, even though I don't know you, because I've been thinking about you lately. I'm very, very sorry to have learned about what happened to your dad. I have a son of nearly your age and another who is 4. The 4-year-old is Marcus and the 8-year-old is James. They are both very cheeky sometimes. (Are you ever cheeky?) But they're very nice boys and I'm glad I'm their dad. They like Star Wars, Pokemon, computer games and football, and they would be happy to watch the television all day and all night if I allowed them to.

Do you ever want to do that? You probably know kids who do. Anyway, what I'm saying is that I'm very lucky to be their father. And the strange thing, Sebastian, is that when I look at James lately, I find myself thinking about you.

I suppose that's the one thing I've learned, a thing my own father told me, when I was 8 or 10, when I was a child of your own age: that we can feel for another and love one another and believe happier times are coming, even when we're in the middle of a hurricane. It's very hard to be brave — I find it hard myself sometimes — any adult who tells you they find it easy isn't telling you the whole truth. But let me say that I know your dad was very brave indeed. And I think I can imagine how proud of you he must have felt, and how he wanted every-thing good and beautiful for you. Knowing that won't make things easier for you at the moment, but, believe me, the day will come when it will. I honestly wouldn't tell you this if I didn't know it was true; but when you're a little bit older, maybe when you're a father yourself, there'll be moments when you think of his bravery and goodness, and in those moments he'll feel very close to you.

People believe all sorts of things about what happens when a loved one dies. But the thing they all believe — every single person in the world — is that in remembering that person and thinking about them sometimes, we somehow discover more about our own selves too. Sometimes, it's painful; I won't tell you a lie. But, then, there are other days when we remember them smiling, or eating, or joking, or walking around the house in their pyjamas, or sleeping, or messing, or cracking a joke; and it's been my own experience, when I've known those losses myself, that it's often the happy recollections that come back to us in the end. When a person we love dies, we're walking through a storm. But on the other side of the sleet and rain and wind, there's a happier and more peaceful place.

We had a painful experience in my own family when I was a good bit older than you — 21 — but even though I was older, I think I know something small of how you feel. It was a sad and difficult time for everyone in my family and, even though she's been gone from me for more than half my life now, there isn't a day when I don't think about her, not in a sad or angry way, but just saying to myself, That was my mum, she wasn't perfect, but she gave me my life, and part of her is in me, and in James and Marcus; as part of her, and part of me, will be in their children eventually. It's an amazing thing to realise. We're all connected. And her loss taught me one thing, which is perhaps the only thing that really matters in the end. We're never alone, even when we're frightened. There are people who love us. They are looking out for us, always. And when we think of that person whose going-away has scared us, some little but powerful thing about them comes back.

So, Sebastian, I wish you the best, and the same to your grandmother, and to everyone who admires you — I have the feeling that's a huge number of people. Well, you deserve every one of them and there are going to be more. I'm one of them. And I always will be.

All warmest wishes,

Joseph O'Connor

Joseph O'Connor

A Dublin-born, award-winning novelist and writer, Joseph O'Connor has received critical acclaim for his novels *Star of the Sea* and *Redemption Falls*, as well as the *Irish Male* trilogy of non-fiction writing. He broadcasts a weekly diary on RTÉ Radio 1's *Drivetime* programme.

Dear Sebastian —

*A good traveller has no fixed
plans and is not intent upon
arriving. — from TAO TE CHING —* ¼ *Bewick*

Pauline Bewick

Pauline Bewick was brought up in Kerry, where she still lives, though she travelled throughout Ireland and lived in caravans, houseboats and railway carriages. Her art is predominantly of nature and demon which often freely intermingle with the countryside of Kerry, Tuscany or the South Pacific. One of the most famous collections is the *Yellow Man* series, which now comprises over 700 objects.

Dear Sebastian,

I hope that you are well. Thank you for allowing me to share a few thoughts with you. As I write this letter, I am remembering back to when I was a young boy of 9 or 10 when my parents took my twin brother and me to the circus. I had always been fascinated with the circus and, being blessed with a vivid imagination, had dreamed of running away and travelling the world as an acrobat or a high-wire juggler.

On that particular day, there was a feast of entertainment with much to enjoy — lions and tigers, knife throwing and fire dancing. But it was the clowns that really stole the show. They had everyone screaming after them as they arrived in a tiny old-fashioned car which they took apart and rebuilt before us in the circus ring. At one stage, one of the clowns leapt out of the ring and came and sat beside us. I can still remember his brilliant bright red tartan suit with huge red shoes and a tiny red bowler hat on the side of his head. His face was painted white with huge black lips and he had a huge red nose. But then I saw something that I will never forget. On the side of his face was a huge big tear. Yes, the clown who was always happy and full of fun had a huge tear on the side of his face. I was stunned. Could it be really true that clowns could cry?

I always believed that only young children and girls cried and certainly not big boys or clowns. Maybe there was something going on inside him that no one knew about. Maybe the circus life wasn't everything I thought it was. As he went back to his friends in the ring, he suddenly turned and waved sadly to me. I hoped that he would be happy.

You see, you never really know what is going on in people's lives. I always believed that clowns were happy and that nothing sad ever happened to them. But, on that day, I learned that you cannot always judge a book by its cover, as we say, or judge people by their outward appearance. What is important, though, is that we have friends who can share our story with us and who will accept us no matter what is going on inside or outside for us. It's no harm to cry and it's no harm to allow others to do the same. As the song says …

'If clowns can cry, why can't you and I …'

With every blessing,

Liam Lawton Rev.

Liam Lawton

Liam Lawton is a composer and performer born in Edenderry, County Offaly. He came to prominence in 2004 having signed with EMI Records, and achieved Platinum status for three of his collections of music. He writes Sacred and Inspirational Music and performs all over the world. He is a priest of the Diocese of Kildare and Leighin and currently resides in County Carlow.

Dear Sebastian,

It is blessedly unlikely that you will have the urge to become a painter. I suppose I, myself, have been more fortunate than most in this respect for the words of the great painter Hilaire Edgar Degas, 'Il faut décourager les arts' clearly did not refer to Art but rather to the artist himself.

At the end of it all, what can I say? What I believe to be important in life is to devote yourself completely to what you are doing.

If you love it, you will be a happy man.

Louis le Brocquy

Louis le Brocquy

Louis le Brocquy

Born in Dublin in 1916, Louis le Brocquy is regarded as Ireland's pre-eminent living painter. A self-taught artist, his work has received much international attention and many accolades in a career that spans 70 years of creative practice. Acknowledged by museum retrospectives worldwide, his work is represented in numerous public collections, from the Guggenheim, New York, to the Tate, London. In Ireland, he is honoured as the first and only living painter to be included in the Permanent Irish Collection of the National Gallery.

Dear Sebastian,

The main thing is to be true to yourself. This implies knowing yourself, knowing who you are, being aware of what your destiny might be. Destiny is everything. Destiny is true freedom, unlike all the freedoms you will be promised, which I promise you will come to nothing unless you are also free in a bigger way. By destiny, I do not mean a preordained course which you cannot change, but a course nonetheless which is your life's journey, in which many of the key decisions will be yours but in which much will happen that is beyond your knowing. We cannot understand this, in the sense of being able to describe it, but we can know it in our hearts, and we can draw on this knowledge by a kind of cradling of the wisdom we have inherited and which lies within ourselves.

Your dad had to leave this life quite suddenly, while still in the prime of his life. But do not think that, before his sudden departure, he did not give you everything you would have got from him if he had lived to be 100. Our society has forgotten how fathers work, what they do, how they convey to us the wisdom of the ages. These things have become invisible to our culture, but they are as strong as ever where they matter: in the love between fathers and sons, fathers and daughters, fathers and the future.

My father died almost 20 years ago, and since then I have come to know him far better than I did while he was alive. When he was merely human, we spoke in a limited language, hampered by mutual misunderstanding, but now I can speak to him in a language that has no limitations except those I cannot help imposing. And the more I speak to him, the more these limits dissolve, the more I grow, so the better our conversations become.

Your dad has departed this 3-dimensional reality we call the world, but I promise you that his presence in your life has truly just begun at the moment of that departure. Think of him, of where he might be, and make this the goal of your existence, your humanity, your personality. This is a simple way of comprehending where your destiny lies, which is to say that it does not lie in anything you can see or touch or describe. But if you can learn to think and be and walk and love in this way – every moment, or as many moments as you can manage – you will be tall and straight like your dad, who sounds to me like a man who knew the true meaning of life. Then you will be fully human, fully alive, fully present every instant of your life. You will smile like your dad all the time, like in that photograph from the newspaper of him standing with his arm around you on a beach. You will know that you are safe, and from this knowledge will come the courage to do things you would otherwise never dream of doing.

Please take this literally. It could be read as mere words, platitudes, nice thoughts to comfort you. My hope in writing this letter is not to comfort you, but to help you to be strong and brave. I want to give you the clue that will lead you to the knowledge of what is infinite in yourself, and so perhaps help you to connect yourself to the Source of all Power, all Hope, all Love.

God bless you all your life,

John Waters

John Waters

John Waters is a journalist who has been a columnist and feature writer with *The Irish Times* since 1990. He is a former editor of both *In Dublin* and *Magill* magazines and has written many books and plays. Among the issues he has championed as a journalist and commentator are the cultural denial of the mutual rights of fathers and children.

James  Galway

Dear Sebastian,

As Shakespeare put it so well, 'it is all in the mind'. He certainly knew what he was talking about as he was an actor, and presumably judged his performance on a daily basis. However, I have reason to believe that in his judgement of his own acting ability, he would have been positive.

I spend part of my day learning new music and it is difficult for me to do, just as it is for anyone learning something new. However, I get on with the job in hand and am happy with each day that shows a little bit of improvement. Don't go looking for a massive improvement in everything you do — learn to delight in small things, because, one day, they will all become the big things you were looking so impatiently for.

Never think badly of yourself, but think positively about how you can make yourself a better person and proceed from there.

Live with what you have. Do the best with what you have.

Have a good life,

Sir James Galway

Sir James Galway

Born in Belfast, Sir James Galway is an author and award-winning flautist nicknamed 'the man with the golden flute'. Since launching his solo career in 1975, he has sold over 30 million albums and has played at the White House, Buckingham Palace, the Vatican and Áras an Uachtaráin.

From: Alison Rosse
To: Christine Horgan
Sent: 04 September 2008 18:09
Subject: Dear Sebastian

Hi Sebastian,

I am not one for making profound statements. All I can say is to listen to your grandmother who is doing all she possibly can to help you, keep the memories of your father, Jordan, alive in your heart, so that, without feeling too much pressure, your actions will never let either of them down. I'm sure you will grow into a fine young man.

Best wishes to you for a brighter future,

Alison Rosse

Lady Alison Rosse

Lady Alison Rosse is a landscape artist and co-guardian, with her husband, of Birr Castle and of the Great Telescope, award-winning gardens and Ireland's Historic Science Centre located within the castle demesne.

17 September 2008

Dear Sebastian,

All I have to say to you is very simple. Whatever work you do, give it your best, put your heart and head into it.

Cherish your friends and value their companionship, their presence. Love yourself as God's creation. Know that life is God's gift to you, a gift you can share happily with others. And don't be slow to give others a hug and a smile.

Every night, as you lie in bed waiting to sleep, talk to your dad and say, 'Dear Dad, I love you.' And, dear Sebastian, may your dreams always be happy.

God bless you always,

Brendan Kennelly

Brendan Kennelly

Oops! Sebastian, I nearly forgot! Balance all your hard work with pleasure and delight. And put all your heart and head into that also – Brendan.

Brendan Kennelly

Brendan Kennelly is a poet and author. Since 1959, he has published over 30 books of poetry, as well as novels, plays, criticism and has edited several collections. He was professor of Modern Literature at Trinity College, Dublin for 30 years until his retirement in 2005.

Hi Sebastian,

There is a great Irish tune entitled 'Contentment is Wealth' and, sure enough, this is true. Finding contentment is another story I suppose, but it is more achievable than we think. When growing up, it is so easy to become bewildered in the task of deciding what you will 'become' and what your choice of work will be in the future.

To this I would ask, What are you happiest doing? What are you very good at? – and start there.

Also when growing up, difficult situations present themselves for us to deal with, and we have choices as to how to deal with them. The correct one is the one you have chosen, in the sense that you have been presented with a very tough loss in your life, and you are coping correctly and are driven by a 'greater spirit' to go forward, be happy, achieve great things and be a positive thinker.

Positive thinking is, and always will be, your trump card.

Steer clear of negative thinking and those who dwell in the negative in any way.

I have been presented with great loss in my life, through the loss of my 3 children who were taken from me 5 years ago. This happened through a split between my children's mother and me. That was her method of dealing with our differences. At the same time, my band De Dannan, that I fronted and managed for 30 years, came to a swift halt.

Severe blows hitting at the same time!

Since then, I have met the most wonderful woman, to whom I am now married. She has an amazing young son, and now I am getting to see my own children, not quite as often as I would like, but I am seeing them and love them so much. My stepson has now 2 brothers and a sister, and my children have a new kid brother!! They get on so well and I am delighted.

Now, I have started an all new line-up to my band, Frankie Gavin & De Dannan, and life is back on track.

In short, Sebastian, life is an amazing adventure. Make it an amazing adventure for yourself.

Reach for the stars.

Be the best that 'you' can at whatever you do. That's all you ever need to expect of yourself. Your own very best efforts, guided by positive thinking and visualising the end results that you personally wish for.

This is what I believe in and try to do every day of my life.

Let every morning be a new and wonderful day. Give thanks for what you do have, and do not complain about what you do not.

Never crave money. If you earn lots of money, that's all very fine, but do not choose a lifestyle for the amount of money you can make at it.

Choose what you are happiest doing and your life will be charmed with good people and many joys.

Sincerely,

Frankie Gavin

Frankie Gavin

Frankie Gavin is a traditional fiddle and flute player from County Galway. When he was 17, he won the All-Ireland Fiddle Championship and the All-Ireland Flute Championship on the same day. In 1973, he co-founded the traditional group De Dannan, which went on to record 16 albums. He has recorded with Sir Yehudi Menuhin, Stephane Grappelli, The Rolling Stones and Keith Richards.

as writing a lot of tiresome old wattle that might make m
great but would not be much good to you. Writing the le
made me realise something a bit humbling for a paren
no expert. My wife and I have three sons, all grown
, decent generous, funny human beings. We are very prou
them but that's the way parents are. The truth is th
y turned out well because of the decisions they made. Ye
y always knew they were loved, as you are, and they did n
e to worry about having a comfortable nest in which
, but they still had important decisions to make. You w
ide what kind of person you will be. A parent can hope a
ourage, but the decision is yours. You will ultimately tak
credit, or the blame, for the man you will become,
ide now on some of your choices. Kind or cruel? Genero
mean? Honourable and honest or crooked and sleazy? A lo
e ago, on a fishing trip with a great and generous friend, w
e chatting after dinner and, in the way adults do after
ple of glasses of wine, I posed the philosophical questio
at's it all about?' To my surprise, he didn't hesitat
at's easy. It's about doing the right thing.' Then, not f
e first time in my life, I deployed my mouth without actua
engaging my brain. I asked, 'How do you know what th
t thing is?' His answer was irrefutable. 'That's the poir
always know what the right thing is.' It's true, and if yo
t the simple, waffle-free philosophy to guide your lif
t's it. The 'right thing' is not always the easiest of mo
venient thing, but you will know what it is, even when
s against the common consensus, perhaps the views of yo
nds. You will know what's right. Your life; your choice. It
y to make mistakes from time to time, so long as you lea
m them. Don't hold grudges. Don't expect anyone else to
fect. By now, your mum and dad will have set your mor
npass and you will know right from wrong. The rest is up
. Have a good life, Sebastian. Do the right thing. I aske
w do you know what the right thing is?' His answer wa
efutable. 'That's the point. You always know what the rig

Politics and State

Oifig an Taoisigh
Office of the Taoiseach

14 October 2008

Dear Sebastian,

At the time of writing this letter, I am serving as Taoiseach
of this nation. That, however, does not qualify me any better
than the next man to pass on advice on how you should
face into the years ahead. What I do have to say comes
from the lessons I have learned, particularly in the teenage
years, when we are eager to learn but perhaps lacking in
the skills to always make the right choices.

For all of us growing up, it is life's experiences and those
around us that, more than anything else, shape us and help
form the adults we eventually become. And given that life's
experiences play such a significant role in our development,
it seems only right that we should take every opportunity
put before us. The simple proverb, Leave no stone
unturned, says it best.

Do not be limited by just those things that you like –
at least sample new and different flavours, sights, sounds
and events, while being mindful to the needs and concerns
of those closest to you. Let your experience be broad and
wide ranging and, over time, you will then be able to

decide what areas bring out the best in you.

Yours sincerely,

Brian Cowen TD

Taoiseach

Brian Cowen TD

Brian Cowen has served as the Fianna Fáil TD for Laois–Offaly since 1984. He has worked in various ministerial posts between 1992 and 1994, and 1997 to the present, serving as Minister for Finance for 4 years from 2004. He succeeded to the leadership of Fianna Fáil and was elected Taoiseach in May 2008.

2 September 2008

Dear Sebastian,

As you grow up you will miss your dad. At times you'll be
under pressure or lonely, in need of advice, and you'll wish he
could be there. At times you'll be angry, asking, Why me?
Why my dad? Unexpected happenings can be so cruel and
difficult to accept, but there's nothing you can do to
change the past.

Don't block out the past, but try to focus on the positives.
Don't let mourning or self-pity become reins that hold you
back from looking confidently to what lies ahead. Always
look to the future, the hope and excitement that it offers
should fill you mind and thoughts. Whatever you do, never
let events of the past, that you cannot control, weigh you
down. It's madness to waste energy and emotion on things
you cannot change.

My father died in an accident when I was literally on the
other side of the world. I was 25, he had given me everything.
I felt robbed. I was robbed. My life changed utterly. Becoming
my own man was fastforwarded, without a father-figure to
impress and consult, I became independent in a way I had
never been previously.

Don't be afraid to think independently or differently, even if
you are told that you are too young to do so... particularly if
you are being told that you are too young to do so.
Conformity is not all it's cracked up to be.

My father liked quotes; one he made me memorise read: 'This above all; to thy own self be true, and it must follow, as the night the day, thou canst not then be false to any man.'

Simple enough: be true to yourself – always – and you won't go far wrong. Knowing right from wrong is rarely difficult, but it's acting on that knowledge that will determine the kind of person you are.

Try to be optimistic, positive. Negative people who see problems and barriers around every corner are dull and never fulfil their potential. Every day you will face challenges of some kind or another: focus immediately on finding solutions. So many people waste so much time, emotion and energy focusing on the detail of a problem and so make solutions harder to find.

Always be true to yourself, that's what is most important. Be positive. Be optimistic. Always love your family, even if they let you down. Be ambitious. Try to fulfil your potential. If you fail at something, so what? – if you've tried honestly. Not to try at all is failure.

God bless you,

Simon Coveney TD

Simon Coveney TD

Simon Coveney is a member of Fine Gael and a TD for Cork South Central. He was first elected to Dáil Éireann in 1998 and was re-elected in the 2002 and 2007 general elections. He served as an MEP for Ireland South in the European Parliament for 3 years from 2004 but, in 2007, had to resign his position when he was re-elected to Dáil Éireann. He is currently Fine Gael front bench spokesperson for Communications, Energy and Natural Resources.

**Department of
Health & Children**
AN ROINN SLÁINTE AGUS LEANAÍ

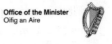

3 December 2008

Dear Sebastian,

I wonder have you seen the film *Jurassic Park*? I remember
when I saw it first I really enjoyed it. I thought the whole idea
of the film was very exciting, the idea that something that had
been extinct for millions of years could still be the life force
behind living animals today. Do you remember the story?

They discovered an insect buried in resin for millions of years
which had dinosaur DNA in its tummy and they used that
DNA to bring dinosaurs back to life. It was as if a magic
formula had been preserved, without degrading at all, which
had allowed something of real value to be restored.

The reason this comes to mind is because I have been
thinking of you and your dad. I've seen photographs of you
together and the love he had for you is clear for all to see.
He has already given you the most precious gift we can give
to one another – the gift of unconditional love.

I have been very fortunate. My parents had long lives.
But I've spoken to many people who lost a parent at a young
age. And they tell me this. Over time it gets harder to
remember exactly what your father or mother looked like.
It gets harder to remember exactly how they spoke or how
they moved. It gets harder to remember a whole range of
things but one magic formula remains unchanged, it doesn't
degrade, it remains a powerful life force – and that's the

secure knowledge the our parents loved us deeply.

As you grow up and go through life, that magic formula will remain perhaps your greatest possession. And it is a possession that you will pass on one day yourself.

It was the love of my parents that gave me the confidence I needed at so many times in my life and I know that your confidence will be boosted time and time again when you reconnect with the love your father has given you.

Yours sincerely,

Mary Harney

Mary Harney TD

Mary Harney was first elected to Dáil Éireann in 1981 as the Fianna Fáil TD for Dublin South-West. In 1985, she co-founded the Progressive Democrats and served as its leader from 1993 to 2006. She also served as Ireland's first female Tánaiste, from 1997 to 2006. She is currently the TD for Dublin Mid-West and is the Minister for Health and Children.

Dear Sebastian,

What motivates me you ask, well, I suppose, I could describe it as the get-up-and-go spirit. The kind of thing that Barack Obama evokes when he tells the cheering crowd, 'Yes we can.' Let me give you an example. A friend of mine, whom I have known for many years, became unemployed as a bus driver. He used to drive the 79 bus. One day, he was watching television and saw a programme about East Timor. He was so upset he founded the East Timor Ireland Solidarity Campaign. His name is Tom Hyland. I helped to get him into the Foreign Affairs Committee where he spoke to department officials and, subsequently, to the minister and indeed several ministers. He went secretly to East Timor and met the imprisoned leader Xanana Gus Mao. What pride I felt when I heard Professor Peter Carey of Oxford say on the BBC, 'Of course, one must accept that in the downfall of Suharto and his regime Tom Hyland of Ballyfermot, Dublin, played a significant role.' Yes, indeed. An unemployed bus man from a marginalised area of one of Dublin's working-class suburbs had put the skids under a skunk of a dictator. That is what I call get up and go. We can all make a difference like Tom Hyland did and as Obama says, 'Yes we can.'

This much I know – you are a damn fool if you let anybody else control your life. It is one thing to be considerate. It's another altogether to become a mere minion at the dictate of a stronger personality. I have made it my business all my life (and mostly successfully) to keep out of the clutches of powerful individuals, groups and organisations.

And, finally, although Sebastian is more *Brideshead Revisited* than *Ulysses* – Happy Bloomsday.

* Extract from *Sunday with David Norris* on Newstalk 106-108 fm

Senator David Norris

Senator David Norris is a politician, writer, broadcaster, conservationist, Joycean scholar and former TCD lecturer. Since 1987, he has been an Independent senator, representing TCD graduates. He was a founding member of the Joint Oireachtas Committee on Foreign Affairs. He was a founder of the Campaign for Homosexual Law Reform and was instrumental in the decriminalising of gay relationships in Ireland in 1993.

BRIAN CROWLEY M.E.P.

PRESIDENT - U.E.N. GROUP

Maryborough Lodge, Maryborough Hill, Douglas, Cork, Ireland.
Tel: +353 (0)21 4896433   Fax: +353 (0)21 4896401
Email: info@briancrowleymep.ie   Website: www.briancrowleymep.ie

15 October 2008

Dear Sebastian,

I know that my words will never make amends for the loss that you feel. However, I hope that, like me, through the support of family, friends and your own innate abilities, you will see that at every turn of life, there is always a new horizon which brings hope and opportunities.

When I was 16, I fell from the roof of a building and I remember, as I fell, seeing the ground come up to meet me. When I hit the ground, I knew that everything would be okay. When I say, 'everything would be okay', I mean that I knew that I could come to terms with, and accept, whatever the consequences of my fall would be.

As I spent 3 months lying in a hospital bed, my faith in Our Lady gave me the confidence to know that, whatever decision or trouble I had to face, firstly, I was not alone and, secondly, that many before me had to overcome adversity and, like them, I, too, would emerge, no doubt changed, but infinitely stronger for the experience. Ever since, each day of my life, I am grateful for the opportunities that I have to meet new people, experience wondrous changes and, most importantly of all, have friends who are ordinary people doing extraordinary things.

Even though, at times, we may all feel down, the support of family and friends will help guide you through. When I went through another difficult period, one of my friends wrote to me and quoted these lines which I always carry with me. I don't know where they come from, but I pass them to you and hope like me, you will be inspired: 'It is better to light a candle than to curse the darkness.'

I wish that you find meaning in these words as well as the same strength of spirit and confidence they gave me.

Stay strong, Sebastian, and stay well. Appreciate the sunshine and the wonder of all the nature that's around you. Take joy in each day. Do this and you will always be sure of the true path to follow.

Kind regards,

Is mise le meas,

Brian Crowley MEP

President UEN Group
Leader FF Group in Europe

Brian Crowley MEP

Brian Crowley was appointed to Seanad Éireann in 1993 when he was still studying law at University College Cork and became the government spokesperson on Justice, Equality and Law Reform. He was elected as the Fianna Fáil MEP for Ireland South in 1994 and was re-elected in 1999, 2004 and 2009.

Director of Communications and Corporate Affairs
An Post
Dublin 1

Dear Sebastian,

Taking time to appreciate the here and now, be it in school, playing sport or hanging out with your friends. If you're aware of what's good in your everyday life, you'll give to and receive more from your studies, your work and all your life relationships.

Put people and truth at the centre of everything you do: systems and technology are wonderful, but without people and without truth, they are worthless.

Always look for the positive in life. There'll be plenty of pressures to think negatively or bleakly at whatever is going on. But I find that if you can get into the habit of looking for the positive in a problem, then the solution is easier to find, and it's not such a pain in the ass.

Be proud of yourself and those close to you, particularly your dad. Treat everyone with respect. It's not always easy, but you'll never regret it.

And after all the advice, just get on with finding your own way through life. We are all on a journey and, as far as we know, we'll only be making it once on this great planet. So see as much of it as you can, and never be afraid to take your own path.

Barney Whelan

> **Barney Whelan, BSc, MBA, FPRII**
> Barney Whelan joined An Post in January 2005 and was appointed director of Communications and Corporate Affairs in 2006. Having spent many years in the aquaculture industry, he was responsible for public relations and brand communications at the ESB. He subsequently held the position of director, Sales and Marketing at the Food Safety Promotion Board. Barney is chair of the Improvised Music Company and CoisCeim Dance Theatre and is a member of the Foundation Board of the National College of Ireland.

Seanad Éireann
Leinster House
Dublin 2

22 July 2008

Senator Feargal Quinn

Dear Sebastian,

Your dad has asked me to give you some advice to help you in the years ahead. I hope these thoughts might give you some guidance as you go through life.

In the old days of the American Wild West, the sheriff was given a 'Sheriff's Star' on his first day of work. This was to help him do his job and he wore it with pride.

I want to give you a STAR. The star I give to you is made up of 4 words.

S The first word begins with the letter S and is for SMILE! You can be generous with a smile – it costs nothing but is priceless in other ways.

It is of great value to wake up each morning with a smile. It starts the morning with a positive belief that it is going to be a good day. In addition, it says to everyone you meet that you are looking forward to the day. It is easy to be flaithiúleach with a smile. People you meet value the smile that you give them and strangers become friends very quickly. Also a smile is contagious – if you smile, people will smile back.

T The T of star is TIME. You can be generous with time. Perhaps there is someone in your family or your class at school who would value a little of your time. It may be a neighbour who lives on their own and finding time to visit or to offer to help in some way may make their day.

I was chairman of the newly created An Post in 1984. We wanted to promote the writing of letters – that was before the days of the mobile phone! We announced that, on the first day, a one penny stamp was all that was needed to post a handwritten letter anywhere in Ireland. It was a great success and millions were posted. We thought that An Post would lose money with this offer because it cost a lot more than one penny to deliver a letter to each home.

However, imagine our surprise 3 days later when there was a huge increase in mail, all at the full rate. You see, people had written to friends and relatives with whom they had lost contact. Those friends and relatives were delighted to receive greetings and felt obliged to reply. So finding time to keep in touch with old friends is something we can all do.

A The A of star is for ATTITUDE. I have a friend, Ito-san, in Japan who is a very successful retailer and I love to visit with him and his family. He came to visit Ireland a few years ago and we took him around some of our supermarkets. As we drove home to dinner, I asked him how he had been so successful – his company had grown from one shop to over 10,000 branches. He reply was, 'Whether you believe you can, or whether you believe you can't, you are right!'

He explained that if he went into a tennis game and said to himself, 'I've no chance against that guy', he was right, he had no chance. However, if he said, 'I can beat that guy', he was also right. In other words, go through life, tennis games or business with a positive attitude and you will find opportunities open to you that would not be available to someone who was always looking on the gloomy side.

R My last letter is R and it stands for RECOGNITION.

Everybody likes to know that their contribution is valued, even if it is only a gesture of recognition. A 'thank you' or a 'good morning' may be only an acknowledgement of a minor favour, but it is nevertheless valued. However, to be able to remember someone's name is a sign of respect that we all value. I would love to have a better memory for names but when I go to the trouble of ensuring that I call someone by their name, I am recognising that they are appreciated.

When I was elected to Seanad Éireann, I jokingly proposed that every citizen should have their name tattooed on their forehead to help me. Every politician I met thought it was a great idea!

Perhaps you have an acquaintance that you meet regularly but have never got to know their name. Don't be shy to ask – just showing that you are interested is a compliment. In Superquinn, we always asked those who worked there to wear a name-badge – and customers liked to call those who served them by name. Once a year, we would ask customers to wear their own names on their lapel so that we could do the same. The butchers and bakers, who were a little reticent about asking regular customers their names, found it easier to learn it that way.

So, it is possible to be generous with those 4 assets that make up the STAR – Smile, Time, Attitude and Recognition.

Remember the quote from the Bible: 'It is more blessed to give than to receive.' (Acts of the Apostles 20:35)

Go n-éirí leat,

[signature: Feargal]

Senator Feargal Quinn

Senator Feargal Quinn

Senator Feargal Quinn is an entrepreneur and businessman who founded the Superquinn supermarket chain in 1960. He was the chairman of An Post from 1979 to 1989 and helped to introduce the National Lottery. He was elected to Seanad Éireann in 1993 as an Independent for the National University of Ireland constitutency. He is author of *Crowning the Customer*.

From: Emily O'Reilly
To: Christine Horgan
Sent: 24 September 2008 12:36
Subject: Dear Sebastian

Dear Sebastian,

I have a daughter who is the same age as you. Her name is Ella. She likes computers, reading, piano, her puppy and *Fair City*. Your dad asked me and lots of other people to write a letter to you but as I haven't met you yet, I'm going to pretend that I'm writing it to Ella as well, if that's okay with you.

Your dad wanted old people like me to advise you on how to live a happy and fulfilled life. When this book is finished, I'm sure you'll read quite a bit of it and I imagine that even though you'll want to be polite about it, a lot of what is written will strike you – as a bright 9 year old – as either boring or preachy (that's when older people tell you what to do) or just talking about things that you don't need to know at this time in your life. I reckon your dad knew all that and that's why he will have made sure that the book is printed on very tough paper so that it will still be around when you're older and maybe what we all say then will seem less boring and less preachy. Although not necessarily ...

The people in this book will tell you all sorts of things about how to live a happy and fulfilled life. If their life has been happy and fulfilled, they will take out the bits that made it so and tell you about them.

But you're not them. You are Sebastian, and how Sebastian lives his life is entirely down to Sebastian. Much of how you will be, and how your life will be, was actually decided about 10 years ago, when you began to grow inside your mum, and your tiny little body – made up of some parts of each of your parents –

began to develop into the unique person that is Sebastian. Let's say your dad and mum were paintbox colours. Your dad was red and your mum was white. You are therefore pink – an entirely different colour even though you are made entirely of your mum and dad. And, of course, nobody else will be exactly the same shade of pink as you. (I realise that pink is a girl colour, but I'm not clever enough to know what colours mix to make blue … Can you even make blue?)

So this unique person called Sebastian will also have a unique experience in this world, because he will experience it and impact on it in a completely unique way. You will enjoy things in a Sebastian way. You will play sport in a Sebastian way. You will decide whether you like toasted marshmallows or not in a Sebastian way. You will choose the people you like in a Sebastian way. You will raise your eyes to heaven when you're exasperated in a Sebastian way. Because, of course, you are Sebastian. You are not, and cannot be, anyone else.

And the great thing about that is that it gives you permission to be yourself. If someone tells you that the secret to a happy and fulfilled life is such and such a thing and you know in your Sebastian soul that you'd rather eat pickled frogs than do such and such a thing, then that's okay. Someone else's recipe is exactly that, someone else's. It's not Sebastian's recipe.

But, Sebastian, what you do have to do, and what your dad I'm sure more than anything wants you to do, is to discover all that there is to discover about the fabulous recipe called Sebastian and make sure that the adult Sebastian cake that emerges from that recipe is the best that it can be. Already, at 9, you will have formed your likes and dislikes, you will have found what you're kind of good at, or not so good at. And one thing that probably everybody in these pages will tell you is that the greatest joy in life is finding something you love and working at it so hard and with so much love that it might even become what you do when you're older and need to make a bit of money.

It took me a long time to find what I was good at. When I was small, I was very shy and couldn't speak properly and that made me even shyer. The speech thing got fixed, but the shyness lasted for a bit and I made that okay by reading lots and writing a bit and then, when I got older, I became a journalist and that made me very happy and very fulfilled. It's a good job I had that small talent because, Sebastian, if you'd ever seen me play basketball or heard me sing, you would have realised that I was a bit of a hopeless case ...

So read the book, take it in, and then, in time, decide for yourself in your Sebastian way what you want to be and what will make you be happy and fulfilled.

And one last thing ... The world can be a bit of sad place sometimes and it's always better if there are people in it who can cheer others up and just be plain nice. Just like your dad. And, no doubt, just like Sebastian.

Love

Emily

Emily O'Reilly

Emily O'Reilly became the Ombudsman and Information Commissioner in 2003, before which she was a journalist and author and had been a political correspondent for various media since 1989. She is also a member of the Standards in Public Office Commission, the Dáil Constituency Commission and the Commission for Public Service Appointments.

John O'Donoghue TD
Ceann Comhairle, Dáil Éireann

Dáil Eireann
Leinster House
Kildare Street
Dublin 2

Dear Sebastian,

I was 8 years of age when my own father died. The loss of my father was a painful loss, and it has to be said that losing a parent is something that we can never fully get over.

The connection we have with our fathers will always be there and we can draw strength from that relationship as we go on to make our own lives.

As we grow and mature and learn to acknowledge and deal with our feelings, we also grow in our understanding of ourselves and how we can live our lives.

As young children, we absorb encouraging words and a set of values from our parents. We can use those values to guide us through our lives in times of uncertainty and confusion.

A father will always want to see his son make informed decisions that will lead to a fulfilling life. He will always want his son to do the work that is needed to prepare himself for the life and the opportunities that are ahead of him.

A father will want his son to believe in himself; to grow in confidence to face the challenges of life; to speak the truth and respect himself and others equally to develop good and worthwhile relationships throughout life.

My family were committed to public service and their community. I have followed them into the world of politics and at the heart of that is the notion that we can do something for others and our community.

People get something back when they contribute to the lives of others.

Many people do valuable work as volunteers. Many people learn to lead and inspire others in their endeavours.

I believe that learning to work well with others and building relationships is very important because most things in life are achieved through working effectively with other people.

I wish you well in the exciting years that lie ahead of you.

Yours sincerely,

John O'Donoghue TD

Ceann Comhairle

John O'Donoghue TD

John O'Donoghue is a Fianna Fáil TD for Kerry South and has been the Ceann Comhairle since June 2007. He has previously served as the Minister for the Arts, Sport and Tourism, and Minister for Justice.

Oifig An Aire Oideachais agus Eolaíochta.
Sráid Maoilbhríde,
Baile Átha Cliath 1

Telefón: (01) 889 6400
Facs: (01) 872 9093

Office of the Minister for Education and Science
Marlborough Street,
Dublin 1

Telephone: (01) 889 6400
Fax: (01) 872 9093

21 November 2008

Dear Sebastian,

I was saddened to hear of the death of your father, Jordan,
from your grandmother, Christine. I extend my deepest
sympathy to you on what is an inestimable loss that has left
a void of great sadness in you life.

I know you will find that your relatives, friends and neighbours
will rally around you and be very supportive and encouraging
to you at this time, in the way your father would wish for you.
This will be of enormous value in helping you to come to
terms with the loss of your father.

However, as it is for everyone, you will come to find your
own way of dealing with your grief privately and, I believe
with that support, positively, always asking, What would Dad
want me to do now? You will find in time that the answers lie
within you, that you will always carry his wisdom and
counsel in your own heart.

You have the memory of your father's dignity and bravery
throughout his illness as an inspiration to you always. The
courageous way in which he faced the greatest challenge of
all is a true example of the selfless love and devotion he held
for you. Through his letters to you, he has ensured that that
memory remains close by always.

I would ask you to remember also, and in particular at those
times you find most difficult, that those we love so dearly,

BATT O'KEEFFE TD   51

remain with us throughout our lives. Love lives on. Treasured memories do not fade when a loved one is no longer with us.

Take heart always, seize every opportunity and live the life your father so dearly wished for you.

Wishing you much happiness always.

Yours sincerely,

Batt

Batt O'Keeffe TD

Minister for Education and Science

Batt O'Keeffe TD

Batt O'Keeffe has served more than 20 years in the Oireachtas as a TD and senator, and was appointed Minister for Education and Science in May 2008. Before that, he was Minister of State with special responsibility in the Department of Environment, Heritage and Local Government. He has served on a number of committees including the Joint Oireachtas Committee on Health and Children, the Public Accounts Committee and the Sustainable Development Committee.

From: Mary O'Rourke

To: Christine Horgan

Sent: 12 November 2008 16:35

Subject: Dear Sebastian

Dear Sebastian,

I do not know if you will be open to taking advice from grown-ups. I remember rearing my own 2 sons and they were never inclined to listen to their elders.

I feel that the poem 'If' by Rudyard Kipling puts into words much of what I would like to say to you. It is a poem still being taught in schools.

If

by Rudyard Kipling

If you can keep your head when all about you
    Are losing theirs and blaming it on you;
If you can trust yourself when all men doubt you,
    But make allowance for their doubting too;
If you can wait and not be tired by waiting,
    Or, being lied about, don't deal in lies,
Or, being hated, don't give way to hating,
    And yet don't look too good, nor talk too wise;

If you can dream – and not make dreams your master;
    If you can think – and not make thoughts your aim;
If you can meet with Triumph and Disaster
    And treat those two imposters just the same;
If you can bear to hear the truth you've spoken
    Twisted by knaves to make a trap for fools,
Or watch the things you gave your life to, broken,
    And stoop and build 'em up with worn-out tools;

If you can make one heap of all your winnings
    And risk it on one turn of pitch-and-toss,

And lose, and start again at your beginnings
  And never breathe a word about your loss;
If you can force your heart and nerve and sinew
  To serve your turn long after they are gone,
And so hold on when there is nothing in you
  Except the Will which says to them: 'Hold on!'

If you can talk with crowds and keep your virtue,
  Or walk with Kings – nor lose the common touch;
If neither foes nor loving friends can hurt you;
  If all men count with you, but none too much;
If you can fill the unforgiving minute
  With sixty seconds' worth of distance run –
Yours is the Earth and everything that's in it,
  And – which is more – you'll be a Man, my son!

The lines which are favourites for me are the first 4 lines of the last stanza.

If you can talk with crowds and keep your virtue,
  Or walk with Kings – nor lose the common touch;
If neither foes nor loving friends can hurt you;
  If all men count with you, but none too much;

May life go well, Sebastian, for you, and I would love to meet you some time.

Warmest regards

Mary O'Rourke TD

Mary O'Rourke TD

Mary O'Rourke was re-elected Fianna Fáil TD for Longford–Westmeath in 2007, having previously served as leader of the party in Seanad Éireann from 2002 to 2007. She was first elected as a TD in 1982 and has held 3 ministerial portfolios, in Public Enterprise and Transport, Health, and Education.

Óglaigh na hÉireann

Oifig An Cheann Foirne
Defence Forces Headquarters
Department of Defence
Infirmary Road
Dublin 7

25 August 2008

Dear Sebastian,

As a young boy, I remember my parents encouraging me and my brothers and sisters to be mannerly and have respect for our elders. On being sent by my late father to collect a message from a friend of his, I waited in his sitting room for some time before getting the package. When my father's friend entered the room, I stood up. Having given me the message, he followed me out to the front door and, as I headed for my bicycle, he called me back.

'In standing up when I came into the sitting room back there,' he said, 'you showed respect for me. That was good manners.' He then handed me a half-crown (a sizeable sum in the late 1950s). Mannerly gestures and actions cost nothing, but the rewards can be wonderful. A smile of appreciation, relief in a face or a simple thank you are rewards that are priceless.

An English churchman, William of Wykeham (1324–1404) coined that wonderful phrase 'Manners maketh Man'. Manners are an indication of decency, of having regard for our fellow human beings, of being aware of those about us, of recognition of those who may need a little help, of respect.

Go n-éirí leat, Sebastian. The greatest reward you will ever get in life is the satisfaction of knowing that you did the right thing.

Dermot Earley
Lieutenant General
Chief of Staff

Lieutenant General Dermot Earley

Lieutenant General Dermot Earley joined the Defence Forces as a cadet in 1965. In 1987, he was posted to the United Nations in New York as the deputy military advisor to the Secretary General. He was appointed the Defence Forces Chief of Staff in April 2007. Lieutenant General Earley had a distinguished early career as a footballer with County Roscommon. He played minor, under-21, junior and senior levels and went on to play in the 1980 All-Ireland final.

1 October 2008

Dear Sebastian,

Starting off in life, it is difficult to take advice, but most of us have learned by bitter experience that it would have been better to learn from others than to make our own mistakes. So I hope that you will forgive me for explaining some of my mistakes.

I used to think in school that sport was more important than anything. My sport was rugby and I put much more effort into it than I put into my studies. This was definitely a big mistake because, even though you are very young when you are at school, if you do not do as well as you can in your examinations, this may affect your whole future. I very nearly failed to get into the Law Faculty in the university that I wanted badly to join and only did so by the skin of my teeth. I learned my lesson and got a good degree but had I failed to become a barrister, my life would have been very different and not at all as satisfying. So try hard. Particularly, try to make the most of your particular talents — and this, of course, applies to other things apart from study (such as sport).

Secondly, recognise the value of good friends and choose them carefully. Friends are nearly as important as family in your life. Now, some people are loners but, in general, I think it is very important to have companions that you can absolutely trust as you go through life. Often, the best of these are the friends that you make when you are young. These friends really know and understand you, so there will be times when their support and advice will be important. I believe that friendship really requires that each party works at it. By this, I mean keeping in touch, confiding in those you trust (and if you don't trust someone, he or she should not be a friend) and listening to and giving advice. In other words, cherish your friends.

Of course, anything that I have said about friends is even more relevant to family. Being close to your family, particularly in the absence of your dad, is vital for your happiness, and indeed theirs. Families, particularly, provide unconditional love and you will need this.

Thirdly, sometimes in life, particularly in career choices, you have to make decisions that involve risk. So, leaving one job to take on another can be risky, but I must say that I took risks and never regretted them. They caused some upset for me and my family in that we had to move abroad on a number of occasions where I would work in completely different jobs, but I think none of us thinks that I did the wrong thing. I have followed the theory that when the ball is at your feet you should generally kick it.

One of the most difficult things in life is recognising how to evaluate yourself because, at the end of the day, knowing the good and bad in yourself is more important than the opinions of others. Many people are very ambitious to achieve things in life but instead of being their own judges of themselves, they rely upon and seek to impress others. You can never validate yourself through the eyes of others – only through your own. I suppose this is why those who try to parade how good they are in any respect are wrong, even though many of us do so from time to time. We all like to be praised, but we should not seek it.

All that I have written is really obvious when you think about it. So also is the final but most important piece of advice that I can give. Doing right and wrong on the serious issues in life ultimately requires choices that should be made through following our conscience. This is easier said than done. Everyone has something in them that tells them what is right and wrong in serious moral choices. Many of us believe that God has given us this moral compass. You should always follow it, not merely because it is the right thing to do but, more immediately, because it is the only way that you will be truly happy.

With all my best wishes,

Yours sincerely,

Peter Sutherland

Peter Sutherland

Peter Sutherland

Peter Sutherland is chairman of BP plc and Goldman Sachs International. He is a former commissioner of the European Communities and a former director general of GATT. He was the founding director general of the World Trade Organisation. Before that he served as attorney general of Ireland and was a member of the Council of State. He served as chairman of Allied Irish Banks and as a non-executive director of many other companies. In 2006, he was appointed by the Pope as financial advisor to the Holy See. He is chairman of the London School of Economics and has received a UK honorary Knighthood and a Chevalier de la Legion d'Honneur, among other honours.

CENTRAL BANK &
FINANCIAL SERVICES
AUTHORITY OF IRELAND

EUROSYSTEM

31 October 2008

Dear Sebastian,

You might expect someone from the Central Bank to write about money – and you would be right! But I have a good reason. You, Sebastian, have a very real connection with money because you were born in 1999, the same year as the euro!

The euro currency was introduced after many, many years of discussion and debate, involving politicians, civil servants, bankers and all sorts of other interested parties. While a lot of that debate was fairly technical and political, the ultimate aim of introducing a single currency was to make life easier for people.

It is hard to imagine now, but one of the more tedious problems associated with going abroad used to be the necessity to ensure that you always had some local currency on you. This went for tourists, students travelling or, because of my job, people like me who had to attend a lot of meetings in places like Brussels. Doing simple things, like buying a newspaper in a shop or paying a bill in a restaurant became a lot more complicated when you realised that you had not brought the local currency with you!

Even though, for a while, the introduction of the euro seemed an almost impossible task, after a lot of meetings and much debate and discussion, the euro finally arrived and it immediately made things that bit easier and better for all sorts of people including the tourist, student or business person.

When we are faced with big, complicated jobs that we don't always want to do or that will require a huge effort, it is often worth thinking about the end result and what that will mean. And, sometimes, it makes these big jobs easier when you can think about the real difference it might make when you get them done.

So, when you celebrate your birthday, remember you share a special year with the euro coin or note in your pocket. And, remember, it was a year when things got just a little bit easier for the 300 million people, including you, who use the euro every day.

Yours sincerely,

John Hurley

John Hurley

A former civil servant, John Hurley became the governor of the Central Bank of Ireland in 2002, having previously served as secretary general of the Department of Finance. He also worked in the Department of Health and served on the council of the ESRI. He is a member of the governing council of the European Central Bank.

Dear Sebastian,

I think that to have a well-informed but open mind is important. You should attempt this with both curiosity and a sense of humour. To have a warm heart is even more important.

We are both in time, as well as out of time. To participate in one's own time with consideration for others is important. The most important things, however, that last are acts of kindness, goodness and generosity. They are timeless and make the legacy of one's life.

Much more important than any accumulation in life is the pursuit of goodness. The possibility of what you can become and what might be achieved with others is what matters. To have sought what is not impossible, what is dreamed of, is and always will be greater than anything suggested as inevitable.

The love of those who went before you will endure and you should remember that in testing times. You are never really alone. And there is beauty, too, to be discovered in so many places, indeed in a myriad of ways all through life.

So be cheerful, strong in courage, generous in solidarity and value the warmth of true friendship. The demands of friendship may be exacting but the rewards are far greater.

Yours sincerely,

Michael D. Higgins

Michael D. Higgins TD

Michael D. Higgins, a former statutory lecturer in Political Science and Sociology at NUIG, is currently an Honorary Adjunct Professor at the Irish Centre for Human Rights. The Labour Party TD for Galway West, he is Labour's spokesperson for Foreign Affairs and was elected president of the party in 2003. He served as Minister for Arts, Culture and the Gaeltacht from 1993 to 1997. He is a writer and poet and noted human rights activist.

Chairman's Office
Córas Iompair Éireann
Tara House
8–16 Tara Street
Dublin 2

Córas Iompair Éireann

26 August 2008

Dear Sebastian,

Below is an anecdote which, in recent years, has had a considerable influence on my attitude to life.

Someone I know very well collapsed in the street and had to have CPR performed at the scene. Such was the seriousness of his condition that the paramedics cracked 5 of his ribs in trying to revive him. Some years later, his philosophy on life is based on one simple truth: If I can dangle my legs over the bed in the morning and put one foot in front of the other and keep moving then I know I'm alive and I have another 'bonus day' in front of me.

Yours sincerely,

John J. Lynch
Chairman

Dr John Lynch
Dr John Lynch is the chairman of the CIÉ group of companies and a former chairman and director general of FÁS.

Theatre, Television and Radio

was writing a lot of tiresome old waffle that might make [
...k great but would not be much good to you. Writing the le
... made me realise something a bit humbling for a paren
...m no expert. My wife and I have three sons, all grown
...w, decent generous, funny human beings. We are very pro
...them but that's the way parents are. The truth is th
...ey turned out well because of the decisions they made. Y...
...ey always knew they were loved, as you are, and they did...
...ve to worry about having a comfortable nest in which
..., but they still had important decisions to make. You...
...cide what kind of person you will be. A parent can hope ...
...courage but the decision is yours. You will ultimately ta...
...e credit, or the blame, for the outcome,
...cide now on some of your choices. Kind or cruel? Genero...
...mean? Honourable and honest or crooked and sleazy? A lo...
...ne ago, on a far-flung trip with a generous friend,
...re chatting after dinner and, in the way adults do afte...
...uple of glasses of wine, I posed the philosophical questio...
...hat's it all about?' To my surprise, he didn't hesita...
...hat's easy. It's about doing the right thing.' Then, not ...
...e first time in my life, I deployed my mouth without actu...
...engaging my brain. I asked, 'How do you know what t...
...ht thing is?' His answer was irrefutable. 'That's the poi...
...u always know what the right thing is.' It's true, and if y...
...nt the simple, waffle-free philosophy to guide your li...
...at's it. The 'right thing' is not always the easiest of mo...
...nvenient thing, but you will know what it is, even when...
...es against the common consensus, perhaps the views of yo...
...ends. You will know what's right. Your life; your choice. I...
...ay to make mistakes from time to time, so long as you lea...
...om them. Don't hold grudges. Don't expect anyone else to...
...rfect. By now, your mum and dad will have set your mo...
...mpass and you will know right from wrong. The rest is up...
...u. Have a good life, Sebastian. Do the right thing. I aske...
...ow do you know what the right thing is?' His answer w...
...efutable. 'That's the point. You always know what the rig...

Dear Sebastian,

I can give you no advice as to how to cope with the death of your father; each person must deal with the death of a parent in his or her own way. But for some more practical advice to do with the handling of life and lifetime situations, I can only pass on some wise words offered to me from time to time and which I've found to be helpful.

First: prepare yourself, the opportunity will come. Whatever it is you want to do with your life, prepare for when the chance arises. When it does, you can then grasp it with both hands. If you've not prepared, but only dreamed of being so, the chance may come 7 times and you'll not be able to take advantage of it.

Second: the greatest fear which people the world over have is having to stand up and address a crowd of people. No matter what you intend to do with your life, no matter what profession you intend to follow, there will come a time when you have to stand up and talk to a bunch of people. It may be because you're captain of the team, or president of the club, or advisor to a group, or Chairman of the Board – you still have to do it. And to overcome the fear of ever having to do it, practise it; join a debating society, a drama group, a musical group, anything, which will force you, now, to start addressing people in a group. If you do not start practising now, when the time comes for you to do it, it will be a nightmare.

Third: don't bear grudges, and do not dwell on real or imagined insults. You cannot control what other people think, or do, or say; you can only control your reaction to what they think or do or say. And regret is a useless, pointless emotion. Yesterday is gone for ever and there is nothing you can do about it or what happened then; much more so last week, last month, last year or 10 years ago. Forget about it. Let it go.

Fourth: that little, niggling, irritating voice that starts warning you that you're about to do something mean or underhanded or sly is your conscience. Good idea to pay attention to it. It's rarely wrong.

Here's to your long, healthy and happy life.

Gay Byrne

Gay Byrne

Broadcaster and well-known personality, Gay Byrne hosted RTÉ's *Late Late Show* from 1962 to 1999 on TV and *The Gay Byrne Show* 1972 to 1999 on radio. He has won a total of 6 Jacob's Awards, the most by one person, for his work in TV and radio. He is currently the chairman of the Road Safety Authority.

From: Eddie Hobbs

To: Jordan Ferguson

Sent: 1 July 2008 15:26

Subject: Dear Sebastian

Dear Sebastian,

Learn to tell knowledge from wisdom – seek people with wisdom, remember that the world is full of the knowledgeable blind. Look for the truth in matters, not just the facts – facts can be misleading. Intelligence comes in many forms as amazing, as diverse as the people you'll meet – see past the narrow measure of IQ and the fascination with money's worth – embrace those with gifts of emotional intelligence, spiritual, sporting, empathy, the list is long. Humility will help you surround yourself with this diversity, working not on your strengths but on what you do least well. Don't look back, reliving old failures over and over – it only brings resentment. Your past, warts and all, is what brings you to this place today, you can't change it, but you can change your future. Avoid the mistake of elevating material gain to the highest level of priority – it cannot bring contentment.

You will inevitably face a moment of extreme testing, your personal Armageddon, when everything you hold is at risk in a moment of darkness. Everybody faces this as least once and how you respond to it will define you as a man. The choices we make define us, not what we say but what we do. Even if the right way is the hardest, take it. It's not how many times you get knocked down but how many times you get back up and fight that will root you to the world. Learn to see with the heart. Treasure your family and close friends because when the dust settles and the measure of life is weighed, it is counted in love – nothing else is of value then.

Eddie Hobbs

Eddie Hobbs

Eddie Hobbs is a financial advisor whose company FDM Ltd acts as an advisor to small businesses. He has campaigned for consumer rights since 1991 when he was director and finance spokesperson for the Consumers' Association of Ireland, a role he performed voluntarily until his resignation in 2006. He is a public speaker, author and TV presenter.

Dear Sebastian,

I have often wondered what I would do if I had to write to my son the letter your dad had to write.

I think I would first want him to know that he was loved above all else – a friend of mine who was moving away from home many years ago said it wasn't being with the loved one that counted, rather knowing that you were loved. I'm sure that knowledge will bring a smile to your face every time you think of your dad.

I'm also enclosing a copy of Desiderata – from the Latin for 'desired things' – it's a poem written by Max Ehrmann in the 1920s, though when we first came across it in the 1970s, we thought it came from a much earlier time! When I was leaving school in 1975, the nuns put it on the back of our Graduation Mass programme. I think it was the best thing they ever did for us and it has served me well since.

I hope you like it,

Eileen

Eileen Dunne

Desiderata
by Max Ehrmann

Go placidly amid the noise and the haste,
and remember what peace there may be in silence.
As far as possible, without surrender,
be on good terms with all persons.
Speak your truth quietly and clearly, and listen to others,
even to the dull and ignorant;
they too have their story.

Avoid loud and aggressive persons;
they are vexatious to the spirit.
If you compare yourself with others,
you may become vain or bitter,
for always there will be
greater and lesser persons than yourself.

Enjoy your achievements as well as your plans.
Keep interested in your own career,
however humble;
it is a real possession in the
changing fortunes of time.

Exercise caution in your business affairs,
for the world is full of trickery.
But let this not blind you
to what virtue there is;
many persons strive for high ideals,
and everywhere life is full of heroism.

Be yourself.
Especially do not feign affection.
Neither be cynical about love,
for in the face of all aridity and disenchantment,
it is as perennial as the grass.

Take kindly the counsel of the years,
gracefully surrendering the things of youth.
Nurture strength of spirit
to shield you in sudden misfortune.
But do not distress yourself with dark imaginings.
Many fears are born of fatigue and loneliness.

Beyond a wholesome discipline,
be gentle with yourself.
You are a child of the universe
no less than the trees and the stars;
you have a right to be here.

And whether or not it is clear to you,
no doubt the universe is unfolding as it should.
Therefore, be at peace with God,
whatever you conceive Him to be.
And whatever your labors and aspirations,
in the noisy confusion of life,
keep peace in your soul.
With all its sham,
drudgery, and broken dreams,
it is still a beautiful world.
Be cheerful.
Strive to be happy.

Eileen Dunne

Eileen Dunne presents the *Nine O'Clock News* on RTÉ 1. She has commentated on many special events, including the papal inauguration in 2005 and for many years announced the results of the Irish jury on the *Eurovision Song Contest*.

Dear Sebastian,

This is the second draft of my letter to you because I realised I was writing a lot of tiresome old waffle that might make me look great but would not be much good to you. Writing the letter made me realise something a bit humbling for a parent: I'm no expert.

My wife and I have 3 sons, all grown up now, decent, generous, funny human beings. We are very proud of them but that's the way parents are. The truth is that they turned out well because of the decisions they made. Yes, they always knew they were loved, as you are, and they did not have to worry about having a comfortable nest in which to live, but they still had important decisions to make. You will decide what kind of person you will be. A parent can hope and encourage, but the decision is yours. You will ultimately take the credit, or the blame, for the man you will become, so decide now on some of your choices. Kind or cruel? Generous or mean? Honourable and honest or crooked and sleazy?

A long time ago, on a fishing trip with a gentle, generous friend, we were chatting after dinner and, in the way adults do after a couple of glasses of wine, I posed the philosophical question, 'What's it all about?' To my surprise, he didn't hesitate. 'That's easy. It's about doing the right thing.' Then, not for the first time in my life, I deployed my mouth without actually engaging my brain. I asked, 'How do you know what the right thing is?' His answer was irrefutable. 'That's the point. You always know what the right thing is.'

It's true, and if you want the simple, waffle-free philosophy to guide your life, that's it. The 'right thing' is not always the easiest or most convenient thing, but you will know what it is, even when it goes against the common consensus, perhaps the views of your friends. You will know what's right. Your life; your choice.

It's okay to make mistakes from time to time, so long as you learn from them. Don't hold grudges. Don't expect anyone else to be perfect. By now, your mum and dad will have set your moral compass and you will know right from wrong. The rest is up to you. Have a good life, Sebastian. Do the right thing.

Every good wish,

Derek Davis
(the one Dustin calls 'Hippo-Head!!')

Derek Davis

Born in Bangor, County Down, Derek Davis is one of Ireland's best-known media personalities. He has hosted numerous programmes on RTÉ, including *The Season That's In It*, *Live at Three* and *Out of the Blue*. He has also hosted the Rose of Tralee competition twice in the 1990s and received 2 Jacob's awards for his TV work in 1984 and 1991. Davis now works with the radio station 4FM, having retired from RTÉ in 2008.

Dear Sebastian,

I really want to begin by saying how sorry I am for the loss of your loving father, Jordan. I, too, lost my mother to cancer and no words can describe how I felt that day, and how I feel still.

I would like to start by telling you a little story that shaped me into the person I have become today.

I began my training to become a ballerina at the age of 14 in an elite ballet school at the foothills of the Ural Mountains in Perm, Russia. I was an average student at everything, including ballet. After a few weeks of training in Russia alongside 10 other Irish girls and boys, a group of Russian students came to watch our ballet class. Understandably, we, the Irish, tried our best to impress, but to no avail. The Russian students spent the next hour and a half laughing out loud at us. I had never been so humiliated in my entire life.

The outstanding memory of that day will always stay with me, and subsequently became my driving force in surpassing my fellow Russian peers in becoming the successful ballerina that I am today. I promised myself that I would never laugh at another person or assume that I am better, faster, stronger or indeed more intelligent than them. It taught me to be gracious and kind, because the tables can, of course, turn on all of us.

Try to turn every negative into the biggest positive, because the people you meet on the way up may very well become the people you will meet on the way down.

Live your life to its fullest and always be happy.

Take care, all the very best.

Monica Loughman

Monica Loughman

Monica Loughman is a prima ballerina who, at the age of 14, studied at the Perm State Ballet School in Russia. On graduating, she was offered a place with the Perm State Theatre and became a soloist in 2002. After completing her teacher training in 2007, she founded the Monica Loughman School of Russian Ballet and the Irish Youth Russian Ballet Company. Her autobiography was published in 2004 and she has featured on many TV programmes, including *Ballet Chancers*.

Dear Sebastian,

Some years ago, I told my very young daughter that, some day, she would think I was the un-coolest human being in the world, and that she would be convinced that I had been put on this earth with the principal objective of embarrassing her. She cried, 'Impossible, that could never happen!' But, of course, it has come to pass, and I have become decidedly embarrassing and un-cool. And that is how it should be; parents and children have to learn to loosen the ties that bind. And every generation has to make that journey from unconditional love through the sometimes sullen and utterly judgemental teens all the way back to unconditional love. As a teenager, I always thought I knew more than my parents, but they were wise enough to humour my delusion.

But some things managed to get through my youthful armour. The most useful words of advice I ever got came from my father.

He said never to bear a grudge, because
you are the bearer, the carrier of that
grudge, the one with the weight on
your shoulders. Often, the person grudged
against is unaware of the grudge you carry,
and sails blithely on through life. So bearing
a grudge is pointless and personally
destructive.

The second piece of advice comes from my
own experience. It is never to look back,
to dwell on what might have been; look
only forward to what still might yet be.

And the final piece of advice I offer relates
to the people I like to be around: learn a
new joke every day and tell it to as many
people as you can! If you can bring a smile
to a face, the world – yours and theirs –
has become a better, brighter place, if
only for a moment.

Finally, may I suggest that there
is no point in looking for the master plan,
no code you can crack, no secret you can
unlock to ensure a happy life. Into
every life a little rain will fall, and each
life will be different. But, in the final
analysis, it is not what you do, but

the way that you do it that makes the difference.

Yours sincerely,

Pat Kenny

Pat Kenny

Pat Kenny is a broadcaster with RTÉ. He hosts a mid-morning radio show, *Today with Pat Kenny*, and hosted the world's longest-running chat show, the *Late Late Show*, for 10 years until May 2009. In September 2009, he launched *The Frontline* a new, weekly, cutting-edge TV current-affairs programme.

RIVER PRODUCTIONS LTD

20 October 2008

Dear Sebastian,

Nothing can ever replace the guidance and love of a good
father. Your dad will always be with you; you are part of him.
When you look in the mirror, you will see him, he will live on
in you.

What would he want for you? Everything you would want
for yourself: a happy, healthy and fulfilled life, being loved by
those close to you and you loving them in return.

I left school at 14 (I am not recommending this to you!), not
knowing what life had in store for me. In an innocent way,
I thought I was special, probably because my wonderful
mother told me I was. I wanted to do something of value in
my life. I was a dreamer and dreamed of being an actor, or
maybe a director or writer, though not knowing then how
to make any of these lofty ambitions come about.

I continue to have a wonderful life, with achievements
beyond my wildest dreams. I've had a great and satisfying
career in the business I dreamed about. I am blessed with a
lovely family. I have 3 sons, Justin, Mark and Danny, and one
daughter, Lucy. The advice I have given them is to be
as good as you can be to everybody you come in contact
with every day, to have fun and to laugh easily and often!
And when the time comes to choose a career, find a job

you love going to every day, something you get pleasure and satisfaction from. You will spend the best years of your life at work – enjoy them!

Believe in yourself. Dream of what you can be – in the words of the song, 'You gotta have a dream, if you don't have a dream, how you gonna have a dream come true?'

Your dad is watching your wonderful life's journey. He will be a guiding light throughout and his love will always live in your heart.

Sincerely,

John McColgan

John McColgan

John McColgan is a theatre and TV director and producer best known for his role in the evolution of *Riverdance*. He is a former head of entertainment at RTÉ Television and at TVAM in London. He is a founding director of Tyrone Productions, one of Ireland's leading independent TV production companies, and is chairman of Today FM. He has also been closely involved with the Abbey Theatre. Among his many awards and accolades, John has received an honorary doctorate from National University of Ireland for his services to the arts in Ireland.

17 December 2008

Dear Sebastian,

My father died when I was 16 years old. There were many things I didn't get to say to him before he left this earth and much that he never got to pass on to me. However, the love he showed me as I grew up forged me into the man I am today and as you read this collection of letters know that if the number of pages in this book actually represented the love your father has for you, it would stretch to many volumes.

I have been truly blessed in my life and have learned numerous lessons since my father passed. I now know that nothing is a matter of Life or Death. It is, in fact, Life and Death — both are part of each other and cannot be separated. It is how you understand this balance and use it to grow which will bring you peace and happiness in the future.

So do not be afraid of death. Or afraid to miss your dad. Do not be afraid to cry. And do not be afraid to ask for help when you feel empty. One day, you will smile when you think of your father, yet that will only come from the love you surround yourself with and reach out for after he is gone.

My dad told me 2 things the year before he died, which I have kept with me to this day. Both were memorable in their simplicity, adaptable in their practicality and, through-out the years, have helped me meet many challenges.

The first was before my stage debut at my school's Christmas concert. I know it is hard to believe but I was actually very shy and really didn't want to stand up in front of everyone and fall flat on my face.

The morning of the show I asked my father for help.

'Lean on the leg that shakes the most.'

At the time, it seemed such a useless, almost pathetic piece of advice. Thanks, Dad. Thanks for reminding me that, later, my knees would be knocking together with fear.

However, that afternoon I actually did lean on the leg that shook the most and it got me through the show without anyone noticing that I was petrified.

It was, believe it or not, a great piece of advice. By focusing on that, it distracted me from worrying about bigger problems, like forgetting my lines or whether the audience would laugh or not.

It was such a simple yet important lesson for all the challenges that came my way later in life – apply yourself only to the things you can control and, in so doing, you will let go of the things you cannot.

That way you can succeed in anything you choose to do, by simply putting your energy into the places you can make a difference.

The second thing he told me that year was this.

'Try to learn by other people's mistakes but, sometimes, you have to make your own.'

Again, so simple. It's something that I have tried so hard to follow in the 20 years since he told me and, yet, many times, have been left picking up the pieces from mistakes I wish I had never made.

However, I know now that he didn't tell me this in order for me to be cautious in life – to sit back and watch while other people fail or succeed and then follow their paths and their dreams as a guide track to my own journey.

He told me this so I wouldn't be afraid to take a chance. So I wouldn't stop reaching for the things in life that I wanted to hold. Even if that did mean falling from time to time.

And he knew that if I learned from those mistakes and kept going, then, one day, I would be the man he knew I was capable of being.

Sebastian, I am still striving to be that man. I still make my own mistakes. I still fall. And I still get up and chase the dreams that I hold dear.

Do not let your dreams be dimmed or your goals be lowered because your father will not be there to share your joy when you do catch them.

Look back and smile when you reach the moments in your life that you wish he could be there to see. It will be his love that will have helped you get to that place. If you do shed a tear, know that he would be smiling and proud. It will help to ease your pain.

Remember do not be afraid to fall: To try something crazy or stretch yourself beyond where you think you are safe. It is only by reaching for your dreams that, one day, they will become real.

And so, Sebastian, that is what I know. For all I have been told in life, and there have been many things, the advice I hold dearest and the lessons that have served me best have come from the man I am proud to call my father.

Be proud of your father, too. By this book, he is giving you a gift for your journey ahead. No one has all the answers but even if you find one inside these letters, then he will have done what he set out to do.

Stay strong. Lean on the leg that shakes the most. Trust me when I tell you that the sun will shine and good days will come again. And know that your father's love will be with you always, whatever path you choose.

P.K. x.

Patrick Kielty

Patrick Kielty

Patrick Kielty is a stand-up comedian from Dundrum, County Down. He began performing in Belfast in the early 1990s shortly after the murder of his father, Jack, by loyalist paramilitaries. He has hosted numerous TV shows in the UK and most recently made his West End acting debut in the Marie Jones play *A Night in November*. He currently lives in London.

From: Darina Allen

To: Jordan Ferguson

Sent: 26 June 2008 20:23

Subject: Dear Sebastian

Dear Sebastian,

1. Try not to let a negative thoughts linger for any length of time in your mind. Thoughts can torment or delight us and we *can* choose.

2. Follow your dream with all the enthusiasm and passion that you can muster. Remember, if you can read, 'you can build a battleship'!

3. When someone is insulting or unkind, we have a choice as to how we react. We can take it to heart, but the anger and resentment are a heavy burden to carry every day. Alternatively, we can let it go and realise it says more about the other person than ourselves.

4. Be slow to judge others, we rarely know the whole story – it's useful to remember: 'Judge not, lest we ourselves be judged.'

5. Share and be generous with both time and possessions, the feel-good and joy factor is worth every penny.

6. Happiness is making time to really connect with your family and friends on a regular basis.

7. Sit down around the kitchen table and share a meal with family and friends.

8. Learn to cook. The way to everyone's heart is through their tummy; it's the easiest way to win friends and influence people.

9. Happiness comes from within. Don't make the mistake of expecting someone or something else to make you happy. It is an unreasonable expectation and will inevitably lead to disappointment and blame.

10. Enjoy each beautiful season and strive to live in the here and now; we can't do anything about the past and the future will take care of itself in due course.

Kind regards

Darina Allen

Darina Allen

Born in Portlaoise, Darina Allen is one of Ireland's best known chefs. In 1983, she founded, and still runs, the Ballymaloe Cookery School. She has appeared on several TV programmes and is the author of many cookery books, including *Simply Delicious* and *A Year at Ballymaloe Cookery School.*

GLORIA HUNNIFORD

Dear Sebastian,

To write about 'guidelines in life' is sometimes a difficult task and, in the end, one can only pass on some nuggets of information which have, over the years, been given by family and friends.

I am going to start with something my mother said, which always amused me and still does. She said, 'In life, you should always have a really good bed and really good pair of shoes, because you're either in one or the other.' How right she was! She also had another simple philosophy about those times when we all find ourselves in a bit of a tizzy. She looked me in the eye and said, 'Now, what can you do about this situation/problem? Can you apologise? Can you mend it? Can you fix it? Can you say how sorry you are over and over? If there's anything you can do, do it 150%, but if the situation is outside your control, let it go, it's negative energy.' Although when I was a child, I didn't think about those philosophies too much, as I get older, I find myself adhering to them constantly, even to this day.

I also think in life, it's very important to give back to those in a less fortunate position. It's important to be good to people but, most importantly, to love and be loved. As my daughter, Caron, wrote in her diary before she died from cancer: 'In the long run all we have is the love of our families and friends.'

I wish you every happiness and success in your life.

Love always,

Gloria Hunniford

Gloria Hunniford

Born in Portadown, County Armagh, Gloria Hunniford is a TV and radio broadcaster. She was the first woman to have a daily show on BBC Radio 2 and has appeared on numerous radio, and TV, programmes. She had her own chat show *Sunday Sunday*, presented BBC 1's *Heaven and Earth* for 2 years until 2007 and now presents *Cash in the Attic*. Her daughter, Caron, died of breast cancer in 2004 after which Gloria set up the Caron Keating Foundation to raise funds for cancer sufferers all over Great Britain. A new series *Angels* for Sky Real Lives starts on 24 July 2009.

Dear Sebastian,

You are lucky to have had such a courageous father who obviously adored you and wanted the very best in life for you.

You are young now, but always remember the most important thing in life is to follow your dreams, and to realise that nothing is impossible.

When people tell you something cannot be done, then you will know you are close to success.

Finally, life isn't about the number of times you are knocked down, but the number of times you get back up.

I wish you a very successful and fulfilled life.

Best wishes,

Michael Flatley

Michael Flatley

Lord of the Dance Michael Flatley, creator of *Riverdance, Lord of the Dance, Feet of Flames* and *Celtic Tiger* is the most successful dance star in history. The first American to win the World Irish Dancing Championship, Michael has performed to over 50 million people in 40 different countries, including over 50 world leaders, and is the only dancer in the world to sell out football stadiums and arenas.

as writing a lot of tiresome old waffle that might make [me]
[look] great but would not be much good to you. Writing the le[tter]
made me realise something a bit humbling for a paren[t]
[I'm] no expert. My wife and I have three sons, all grown [up]
[now], decent generous, funny human beings. We are very pro[ud of]
them but that's the way parents are. The truth is th[at]
[the]y turned out well because of the decisions they made. Ye[s]
[the]y always knew they were loved, as you are, and they did n[ot]
[hav]e to worry about having a comfortable nest in which
[to], but they still had important decisions to make. You w[ill]
[dec]ide what kind of person you will be. A parent can hope a[nd]
[enc]ourage but the decision is yours. You will ultimately ta[ke]
the credit, or the blame, for the [outcome],
[dec]ide now on some of your choices. Kind or cruel? Genero[us or]
[mean]? Honourable and honest or crooked and sleazy? A lo[ng]
[tim]e ago, on a fishing trip with [a friend] ... and w[e]
[we]re chatting after dinner and, in the way adults do after [a]
[cou]ple of glasses of wine, I posed the philosophical questio[n]
[wh]at's it all about?' To my surprise, he didn't hesitat[e]
[wh]at's easy. It's about doing the right thing.' Then, not f[or the]
[the] first time in my life, I deployed my mouth without actua[lly]
[en]gaging my brain. I asked, 'How do you know what th[e]
[righ]t thing is?' His answer was irrefutable. 'That's the poin[t]
[you] always know what the right thing is.' It's true, and if y[ou]
[wan]t the simple, waffle-free philosophy to guide your lif[e]
[tha]t's it. The 'right thing' is not always the easiest of mo[st]
[con]venient thing, but you will know what it is; even when [it]
[i]s against the common consensus, perhaps the views of yo[ur]
[frie]nds. You will know what's right. Your life; your choice. I[t's]
[ok]ay to make mistakes from time to time, so long as you lea[rn]
[fro]m them. Don't hold grudges. Don't expect anyone else to b[e]
[per]fect. By now, your mum and dad will have set your mor[al]
[com]pass and you will know right from wrong. The rest is up [to]
[you]. Have a good life, Sebastian. Do the right thing. I aske[d]
[ho]w do you know what the right thing is?' His answer wa[s]
[irre]futable. 'That's the point. You always know what the rig[ht]

Church, Charity and Medicine

June 2008

Dear Sebastian,

Your father, Jordan, when he realised the seriousness of his illness, asked me and a hundred others to write a letter of advice to you. He is your father, he loves you deeply, he's proud of you. More than anything, he wants your life to be a success. In times of doubt, read your dad's wisdom. It's a priceless gift to have.

In the immediate future you will need time for grieving. Take it, don't rush it. There will also come a time when you will have to face the world yourself. This would have happened even if your father had lived a long life. Every mature young person has to face that decision. It is part of growing up.

For me, it is a privilege to be asked to write to you, Sebastian, but it is also an awesome responsibility. I've spent 10 days praying and thinking about it. I have decided to write now, otherwise I will become paralysed by my own confusion.

In his letter to me your dad suggested that I should try to pass on practical tips to you to help you through the trauma of his serious illness and that I should share experiences from my own life.

So, Sebastian, let me begin by saying that I am really sorry to learn that your dad is so ill whilst still a young man. I have been praying, and will continue to pray, that you will have the strength to cope with whatever happens and that your family will be blessed with healing in your lives. I have been praying for your dad, your mother, and especially for your dad's parents who are looking after him. May your family find hope during these trying times.

That, in itself, will be a life-giving experience for you. You'll learn more from being with your family in times of trouble than you will from any book. Those memories will be an anchor for you in the stormy seas of life.

Your dad says that you have a wonderful mum, caring grandparents, good friends and that you attend an enlightened school. There are many gifts and blessings there and, once again, you will learn valuable lessons from those sources.

One of the most difficult obstacles I had to overcome in writing to you is the fact that I am an unmarried Catholic priest, with no children of my own. I feel totally inadequate. I don't have the confidence to write to a 9-year-old boy facing life without his father. This played so heavily on my mind that I asked those attending Masses in our church to help me. I particularly asked dads of young families to help me. I wouldn't want to say anything which would be hurtful, useless or too upsetting.

Here's how some of those people helped me. They will keep you in their prayers, not just now, but into the future. They say your mother's love will support you in a special way and will help fill the void left by your father's untimely death. They reminded me that every child eventually has to learn to face the world alone, even when both parents are still alive.

One of those who wrote pointed out that whilst advice is helpful and well-meaning, it comes from fallible human beings who constantly make wrong choices themselves. In other words, be careful not to take our advice too seriously. It is best to stand on your own 2 feet and learn, gradually, to make your own choices as you grow in wisdom and knowledge.

A couple of people suggested I pass on this line from Desiderata. 'You are a child of the universe, no less than the trees and the stars, you have a right to be here.'

When you read this book of letters there is a danger that your life will be overloaded. Don't let it do your head in. Sift through it for whatever is helpful. Discard the rest. Don't try to live up to our expectations. You must make important decisions, for the present, with your mother. Grieve in the best way you can. But laugh and be happy, too, whenever the opportunity arises. Some days you will remember your dad, more days you won't. The special days in your life will remain special days, even though they will be tainted with a certain emptiness. You will learn how to cope, when to remember and when to get on with life.

Sebastian, don't fall into the trap of trying to do what you think your dad would have wanted you to do. The world will change and all advice will be outdated in a few years.

You'll have to face a different world and if your father had lived, he too would constantly update his view of life. So don't get stuck in a time-warp.

I was in my late teens when my mother died and I can tell you that over 40 years later, I still miss her. It angered and upset me at the time. Gradually, though, I realised that even though I could not see my mother, I could feel her presence in my life. Don't ask me to explain how that happens, I just know that she is with me, even now. I would never have been a priest had not my mother guided me from her place close to God. I still pray to her and she helps me every day in life. I know your dad loves you just as much as my mother loved me. A love like his will never die.

I believe in life after death and I hope you'll hold on to enough faith to know you'll meet your dad again.

As a priest, I have been with many families who lost a young parent to death. It is always sad and difficult. Nothing ever replaces our parents. Yet, I admit that in the vast majority of cases, families survived brilliantly and grew up to be caring, giving, well adjusted, selfless people. We can over-come many obstacles in life when we work together, help one another as best we can, and allow others into our lives to help us.

Sebastian, work hard at finding out what your own unique gifts are. You will discover that your best gifts now may not be your best gifts 10 years hence: keep searching; keep questioning, keep growing. Without your dad around, you could become too dependent on the approval of others.

For a long time, I tried to be a 'people pleaser' and it almost destroyed me. With the help of friends, I was able to discover my own humanity and, after that, some integrity. Which, in turn, gave me the strength of character to be true to myself, leading eventually to the greatest gift of all, a sense of fulfilment and inner peace.

Sebastian, you are going through the most difficult part now. Everything is uncertain and the unknown is frightening. I heard your dad say on radio that you are a mature young man. I'm sure your mother and your family will help you to cope with whatever happens.

But I suspect (and hope) that you will soon realise that even though all of us are well-meaning people, what helps you most is not our advice but our prayers, our attempts to understand your feelings, our concern and our genuine love for you.

If, in the future, you might want to contact me, don't hesitate to do so. I promise to pray for you every single day. God bless and guide you.

Sincerely,

Brian D'Arcy CP

Fr Brian D'Arcy

Fr Brian D'Arcy is a popular Passionist priest from County Fermanagh, where he serves as rector at The Graan in Enniskillen. He has written a column for the *Sunday World* newspaper since 1976 and is the host of BBC Northern Ireland's weekly radio programme *Sunday With Brian D'Arcy* and BBC Radio 2's *Sunday Half Hour*. He has been broadcasting 'Pause For Thought' on *Wake Up With Wogan* for 20 years now and has also published 12 books to date.

From: Fergus Finlay

To: Christine Horgan

Sent: 25 September 2008 16:23

Subject: Dear Sebastian

Dear Sebastian,

A few years ago, all of us in the family went to support my daughter, Mandy, in the Special Olympics World Games in America. Mandy was born with Down Syndrome and in the hospital when she was a baby, the doctor said to us, 'Just take her home. She'll never amount to much, but she'll never give you too much trouble.' That doctor was wrong on both counts – Mandy became the first member of her family to represent Ireland and she is perfectly capable of giving trouble!

While we were there at the Special Olympic Games, we went to see the athletics. And we had an experience at one of the heats in the 1,500 metres that I'd like to tell you about.

They were lining up for the event as we took our seats. In the outside lane, so close to us I could see his eyes, was a black athlete. The eyes were dull, slightly unfocused. He had an intellectual disability. And he had only one leg – he was using an old-fashioned wooden crutch.

He was slower than all the rest to start and, by the end of the first lap, it was clear that he was in trouble, without the remotest chance of qualifying for the next round. By the time 7 of the 8 competitors had finished the heat, he still had more than a lap to go. And he was wobbling badly.

But he never stopped. More than that, he never faltered. Although, from where we sat, it looked as if each step was more painful for him than the previous one, he was determined to finish.

And little by little, it became clear that the entire crowd was determined to help. As he eventually crossed the line, collapsing in to the arms of his coach, 2,500 people gave him a standing ovation. None of them, I'll bet, could remember who had won the heat. And none of them will ever forget the way that African athlete overcame the day.

Do you know what that athlete had? It's a big word – resilience. Mandy has it too. It means that no matter how tough things get, you have something inside you that helps you to keep going.

And do you know where resilience comes from? It comes from love, and from the memory of love. When you get a bit older, read some of the stories that Charles Dickens wrote – about Oliver Twist, Tiny Tim, Nicholas Nickleby and others. They all had terrible times in their lives, and they all got through it because, once, someone loved them and they never forgot that.

There is no memory that lasts as long as the memory of being loved. And it's very clear to me, Sebastian, that a lot of people love you. And you can store up for ever the memory of the love your dad had for you. You'll see it in any photograph of you and him together, and in the letters he has left you. And I hope you'll find it in this book. You can build an awful lot with the memory of love and the experience of love. So treasure it, and you'll be great.

Fergus Finlay

CEO, Barnardos

Fergus Finlay

Fergus Finlay is CEO of Barnardos, Ireland's leading children's charity. Most of his previous career was in politics – he served as an advisor to Dick Spring, leader of the Irish Labour Party, from 1983 until 1997, and to the subsequent leader, Pat Rabbitte. He is a weekly columnist with the *Irish Examiner*, broadcasts a weekly radio column on RTÉ's *Drivetime*, and has published 4 books. He helped to organise the 2003 Special Olympics World Games in Ireland and is involved in the disability movement.

Diocese of Cork and Ross

www.corkandross.org

Diocese of Cork and Ross
Cork and Ross Offices
Redemption Road
Cork

Dear Sebastian,

Firstly, I sympathise very sincerely with you on the death of
your father, Jordan. Obviously, you had a very great relationship
with him. He is still very close to you now – indeed your
relationship with him is deeper and the distance less than
when he was alive. This has been my experience also. My
father died 10 years ago and I feel very close to him now.
I feel very much his loving presence. I am certain that this
will be your experience also, and that your father will continue
to inspire you. We know, too, that those who have gone before
with us are happy with the Lord. In the Bible, Jesus tells us
that in His father's house there are many mansions and that
He is going to prepare a place for us. In other words, He says,
that, in heaven, there is room for all. Your father, Sebastian, is
enjoying that special place.

Your father was a very unselfish man. He was thinking of you
and your welfare, particularly during his illness. I think also
that despite the heavy cross that he was asked to carry, he
was a very happy man. He died peacefully, knowing that he
had done everything for you. Indeed that concern for others
and the desire to help in any way is the secret to happiness.
Many people today are searching for happiness. The search
for happiness is one of the most constant pursuits of the
human heart. It gives energy to most of what we do.

People today ask themselves these questions: Am I happy? Is there joy in my life? Does anyone love me? These are valid questions but they are not the right questions. They are a result of something else. That something else is precisely our effort to bring joy, love and meaning into other people's lives. We earn things only by giving them away. We should ask ourselves these questions and I am certain your father asked himself the same questions: Do I try to make people happy? Am I constantly trying to love others more deeply? Do I try to bring joy and peace into other people's lives? That is what your father tried to do and he is therefore a great role model for you.

I know, Sebastian, that you, too, will continue to reach out and help others, especially those who are suffering in any way. After Jesus had washed the feet of His disciples the night before He died, He turned to them and said, 'Happiness will be yours if you act accordingly.'

I remain,

Yours sincerely in Christ,

+ John Buckley

+John Buckley
Bishop of Cork and Ross

Bishop John Buckley

Bishop John Buckley, a native of Inchigeela, County Cork, was ordained to the priesthood in 1965, having studied at St Patrick's College, Maynooth. He was ordained the titular bishop of Leptis Magna and auxiliary bishop of Cork and Ross in 1984 and was installed as the bishop of Cork and Ross in 1998. He is a member of the Irish Episcopal Conference and is the chairman of the Bishops' Commission on Healthcare/ Disabilities/ Drugs.

May 2008

Dear Sebastian,

It is a privilege to share some thoughts with you as one who has spent my adult life in service of the Church of Ireland and the life of our country.

1. Enjoy your faith in a God of love and forgiveness. Never let your faith be a burden — let it be a joy and a privilege.

2. Enjoy those around you — they are all different but like you are made in the image of the one God.

3. Never judge others without also feeling compassion for them. Remember, they to will have opinions about you!

4. Try each day to do something, no matter how small, to make life easier for someone else.

5. Learn that forgiveness is one of the most important gifts we have in life.

6. When you have a home and family of your own, one day, make it as happy a place as you can where everyone who calls is made welcome.

+ Robin Eames.

Archbishop Robin Eames

Archbishop Lord Robin Eames

Archbishop Lord Robin Eames was the Church of Ireland archbishop of Armagh, Primate of All-Ireland, from 1986 to 2006. He currently sits as a cross bencher in the House of Lords after being announced as Baron Eames in 2005. He has received numerous awards and honorary doctorates.

Irish Guide Dogs for the Blind
National Headquarters &
Training Centre
Model Farm Road
Cork

irish guide dogs
for the blind

23 September 2008

Dear Sebastian,

Firstly, I consider the request from your Granny Christine an
honour and a privilege, to contribute a little about myself, in
respect of your dad Jordan's wishes to have a book published, containing the lives of a variety of men and women,
some very ordinary, like myself, and others who have
reached international status in their chosen careers.

As a 10 year old, I was extremely interested in all types of
sports, particularly the game of rugby and this continued in
playing capacity right up until I lost my sight in a sporting
accident at the ripe old age of 30 years. I mention sport as,
after my accident, it formed a very important part of my life.
Apart from learning to accept losing along with winning, it
also toughened me up, for many the challenges, which I, like
many others, had to ensure during our lifetime.

From an early age, I was always very ambitious and never
accepted the word 'failure', I was not always a winner, but
my expectation was always to succeed. Before I lost my
sight, I was married with 2 children, I was operating a highly
successful business in the motor industry, playing rugby, and
I believed the world was my oyster.

Suddenly, I suffered immediate sight loss and everything

came crashing down. This misfortune was multiplied, when a senior consultant told me that I would be of great assistance to my wife in our home. At this juncture, I really felt on the scrapheap. However, after reflecting for a short period, on what he had said, I decided that I would prove him wrong and I realise now that instead of being a complete downer, his comments acted as an incentive. My first priority was to regain my mobility, in order that I could move about independently. However, there was more bad news, when I found that there was no mobility training in our country.

Fortunately, I was accepted for training at a rehabilitation centre in Torquay in Devon. I was amazed at the magnificent facility and the high quality of the training. I realised then that there was life after blindness, but I felt ashamed regarding the total lack of such a facility for my fellow blind in Ireland and pledged that I would move heaven and earth to have such a mobility centre established in my own country.

Today, that mobility training centre has flourished and many blind have gained for the first time their mobile independence and, in 2005, the association introduced the Assistant Dog Service where children with autism have increased their quality of life for both themselves and their families. All the credit for the establishment of these vital services must go to our volunteers and the enormous generosity of the Irish people, who provide 85% of our annual core funding.

I also believe that my social contribution, brought success to my continuation in the motor industry, where I was fortunate to provide employment for 60 employees.

Finally, Sebastian, I understand that your dear dad, mum and granny are made of tough stuff, full of ambition and not afraid of challenge. Therefore, you have the very same in your genes and I know that you have an extremely bright future ahead of you.

Kind regards and best wishes for a successful launch of this special publication and delivering on Jordan's final wish.

Yours sincerely,

Jim Dennehy

Jim Dennehy

After losing his sight in a sporting accident when he was 30, Jim Dennehy (along with Mary Dunlop) established the Irish Guide Dogs for the Blind in 1976 and is currently president and director of the organisation. The organisation started the Assistant Dog Service to help children with autism, in 2005. In 2006, after 50 years in the motor industry, he retired as managing director of Dennehy's Cross Garage in Cork.

Dear Sebastian,

The best advice I can give to you is that you try always, even when it is very difficult, to *look for the beauty*. What do I mean by this? We all live in a world which is obsessed in looking for the ugly, the mean and the cruel in others and in the world itself. Even when someone does a genuinely good or kind thing for another person, there will be plenty of people around who will look for a hidden motive, which they assume will be neither good nor kind. But there is beauty to be seen and found everywhere, if we could only develop the eyes and souls to see it.

There is, of course, beauty in the physical world, a beauty which we can so easily overlook. There is beauty to be encountered in music, or in art, or in poetry. But, most important of all, there is true and profound beauty to be found in people. Very few people may be supremely physically beautiful in every respect (and this almost certainly won't last for too long!) but there is a deeper beauty to be recognised in virtually any other person – it may be a warm smile, smiling eyes, or an attractive voice, but it may also be a real generosity of spirit, an encouraging personality or total dependability. If one always looks for the beauty rather than the ugliness, then life is not only happier but it is also far more fulfilling. We respond to beauty with a generosity and unselfishness from within ourselves.

Finding the beauty that is there in the physical world, in the arts and, most importantly, in people brings us into contact with the eternal – that which is above and beyond our little lives – and by doing this, I believe it may help us to find our link also with God, even at times when we may feel forgotten by Him. There are times when my religious faith has been held together by looking for the beauty in what God has made and which He loves. It is too easy to be cynical and to look only for what is ungenerous and cruel. Look for the beauty, and you may find yourself face to face with God.

God bless you always, Sebastian,

+Richard Clarke

Bishop of Meath and Kildare

Most Reverend Bishop Richard Clarke

Bishop Richard Clarke has been the Church of Ireland bishop of Meath and Kildare since 1996. He is chair of the Church of Ireland Commission for Christian Unity and Dialogue.

FOCUS
IRELAND

Everyone has a right to a place they can call home.

12 September 2008

Dear Sebastian,

In the Book of Ecclesiastes we read:

There is a season for everything

A time for every occupation under heaven

A time for giving birth

A time for dying ...

A time for sowing ...

A time for reaping ...

A time for living ...

A time for peace ...

This is your time, Sebastian. This is your life.

The model that Christians are given for living is the life of Jesus. Jesus risked everything. He was abandoned, rejected, betrayed and killed for being who He was, for saying, doing what He did in His time. He was crucified for asking the right questions of the right people and for standing up and taking responsibility for the right things in His time. This is what it means to be born to the world, to break what is false and what is hidden and destructive in our time.

It is not easy but there are great spiritual comforts for us if we are willing to become people of truth in our time, however hard that may be. To live with honesty and integrity, letting go of falsity, gives us a new sense of freedom and truth. Once we have broken through the pretences, the barriers, the falsities that blind us and bind us, we are free, we are free for ever and no one can ever take that freedom from us.

With freedom, truth, honesty and integrity comes self-esteem. Self-esteem is something that, once truly acquired, we can never lose. As Dag Hammarskjöld said, 'Life only demands from you the strength you possess. Only one feat is possible – not to have run away.'

When we have done what we must do, what we were put here to do at this time, in this place, we become who we are called to be and nobody can take that from us. However hard life may be, however difficult its stresses and pressures, even if we appear to fail and people leave us and reject us and disown us, we will never die before we have lived our lives to the full and, even in death, we will live on in the minds and hearts of those who follow us.

I hope my contribution will somehow help you on your life's journey.

God bless you,

Stan

Sr Stan

Sr Stanislaus Kennedy

Sr Stanislaus Kennedy is an Irish Sister of Charity and one of Ireland's best-known social innovators. In the 1980s, she founded Focus Ireland, of which she is life president. In the 1990s, she founded and is director of the Sanctuary. In 2001, she founded Social Innovations Ireland out of which she founded The Immigrant Council of Ireland and Young Social Innovators. She is director and chairperson of both organisations. She is a board member of the Community Foundation for Ireland and is also the author of several bestselling books.

From: Tommy Morris
To: Jordan Ferguson
Sent: 27 June 2008 13:38
Subject: Dear Sebastian

Sebastian,

What a tremendous opportunity this is for me to share with you some thoughts. I recall my younger years and hoping that my independence would hurry up. Now, looking back, I have very few regrets to mention, yet wonderful memories.

But I was always excited with the expression 'I would rather burn out than rust'. I heard this when I was asked by my brother, Richard, to be his sponsor at his confirmation ceremony. The bishop speaking at the end of the service used those very words along with 'make a difference' and they stuck with me.

You, Sebastian, you can make a difference and that difference may be highlighted, it may influence leaders or even change the world. But, more likely, it may be simple, it might even go unnoticed. But you will know in your heart that you are making a difference.

Climbing the hill of life is a journey with challenges and joy. But, do stop now and again. Look back, enjoy the vista, rest for a while, think of those who have gone, get excited about those who are coming. Check the map. Share the map, ask for direction or help those who could be lost. But always remember *you* can make a difference.

Enjoy this journey,

Tommy Morris

Tommy Morris

Tommy Morris was reared in Ballyfermot, Dublin. He was bereaved at 15 years old when his father died of a protracted illness. He is a medical social worker at Our Lady's Hospice in Dublin where he works with families and the terminally ill as part of a committed Hospice Home Care Team.

Dear Sebastian,

I'm sure it must be very difficult for you not having your dad around any more. But our parents do not necessarily need to be physically beside us to be 'with' us — they can be with us in many ways and one of these is through the influence that they have on how we live our lives, even years after they have gone. By passing on their values, they continue to live on in us and to be an inescapable part of our lives.

My mother was a very loving and powerful woman, even though she was only 5 ft tall. When I was a child, a man called 'Johnny the Cans' walked the lanes and boreens of East Cork where I lived, looking for food and shelter. He was homeless and every few months came to our parish where he was well known. He was called Johnny the Cans because he had tin cans, cups and saucepans somehow attached to a leather belt swung round the waist of his overcoat — these were his only possession. He asked for money, cigarettes and food and the neighbours treated him with kindness —

he was clean, quiet and harmless and, at night, was believed to sleep in people's barns even though nobody ever saw him. One summer day, he knocked on our door and my mother asked him if he would like to come in for something to eat. Unusually for Johnny, who always liked to take away the food he was given, he said yes, he would come in. I remember he asked me what school I went to and we chatted briefly while my mother got out a linen tablecloth and our white china, and set the table. She put a serviette on his plate and served him freshly made sandwiches and cake.

By those simple actions my mother taught me valuable lessons – every person is deserving of respect, deserving of china and serviettes, from the lowliest to the greatest. My mother showed that Johnny's status in life as a homeless man did not deter her from treating him like a visiting dignitary, for a few short minutes of his hard life. As she often said in her compassion for her fellow humans, 'He is somebody's son, too.'

Her values, I hope, live on in me and in this way part of her still exists in this world. Your dad will live on in a similar way, Sebastian.

Yours,

Patricia Casey

Professor Patricia Casey

Patricia Casey is Professor of Adult Psychiatry at University College Dublin and a consultant psychiatrist at the Mater Misercordiae Hospital in Dublin. She has written 5 books and is a columnist for the *Irish Independent*. Professor Casey is also well known for her conservative stance on social issues.

GOAL
Dún Laoghaire
County Dublin

30 September 2008

Dear Sebastian,

You have inherited a special gift to be able to look after
this world and see the good and not the bad things.
There is a solution to every problem, if your heart is big
enough to find it.

You have lost someone so very dear to you that life must
seem extraordinarily unfair. And it often is. Nothing you will
do will in any way compensate for the shocking void in your
life. But inside you is a strength which may prove to be your
daddy's lasting gift. When you need it and dig beneath the
surface, it will get you through the darkness. Many other
children have recovered from such pain and they should
give you hope.

In offering a helping hand to those whom you clearly know
need it, you will be paying the greatest respect possible to
your father. I'm sure you want him to feel proud of you, and I
believe that, and I'm speaking as a parent and a grandparent
now, there is nothing more important to a parent than to be
aware that his or her child is taking the sort of action which
can brighten the lives of others.

You worry about people who are hungry and people who
have no education, and wonder why the international

community isn't responding. That I can tell you is a thought that has seen me through many a sleepless night.

Let me explain. In 1984, I had just returned from the Ethiopian famine – the worst famine of the century where 6 million people were dying of starvation. I was very eager to get my message across so that more assistance would be brought to bear on the situation – but I wasn't being very successful and I knew that organisations like GOAL could do very little given our size.

I remember speaking to a group of 7 to 8 year olds in a school in Skerries and after I had shown my little film of slides to the children of the tragedy that was Ethiopia at the time, one little boy stood up and said, 'Mr O'Shea, my daddy is a fisherman and he has a boat. He will go to Uthopia [he couldn't pronounce Ethiopia properly] and load up the boat with hungry children, bring them to Skerries and feed them and send them back when there is food in Uthopia. Lots of the other lads' daddies are fishermen as well and they have boats and I'm sure they will go as well.'

Sebastian, this suggestion was infinitely more sensible than anything the international community was doing for the people of Ethiopia at the time. It proved to me again that love – genuine love – beats in the hearts of children and if that love can somehow be implanted in the hearts of world leaders, we would not have the degree of suffering that we have today and have had for generations.

I know you will share your life with others, especially with others less fortunate than yourself. There is no word, Sebastian, to describe the happiness and joy which will float to you from showing a genuine interest in those less fortunate than yourself.

Good luck to you, Sebastian, and God bless,

John O'Shea

CEO GOAL

John O'Shea

John O'Shea is the founder and CEO of GOAL, the Third World relief and development agency. He is well known as a humanitarian and his awards include the 2005 Ernst & Young Social Entrepreneur of the Year, the 2004 Tipperary International Peace Award and the 1995 Texaco Outstanding Achievement Award. He is a former sports reporter with the Irish Press Group. He holds honorary doctorates from Notre Dame University and the Open University.

as writing a lot of tiresome old waffle that might make m
great but would not be much good to you. Writing the le
made me realise something a bit humbling for a paren
no expert. My wife and I have three sons, all grown
, decent generous, funny human beings. We are very pro
them but that's the way parents are. The truth is th
y turned out well because of the decisions they made. Ye
y always knew they were loved, as you are, and they did n
e to worry about having a comfortable nest in which
, but they still had important decisions to make. You w
ide what kind of person you will be. A parent can hope a
ourage ut the decision is ours. Y u will ultimately ta

Business, Finance

cre the me,
ide ow on some of your choice. Kind or cruel? Genero
mean? Honourable nd h st or cr ked and sleazy? A lo
e ago, on strip a g tle us friend, v

and the Law

e chatting after dinn r and, in the ay adults do after
ple of glasses of wine, I posed the philosophical questio
at's it all about?' To my surprise, he didn't hesitat
at's easy. It's about doing the right thing.' Then, not f
first time in my life, I deployed my mouth without actu
engaging my brain. I asked, 'How do you know what th
t thing is?' His answer was irrefutable. 'That's the poin
always know what the right thing is.' It's true, and if y
t the simple, waffle-free philosophy to guide your lif
t's it. The 'right thing' is not always the easiest of mo
venient thing, but you will know what it is, even when
s against the common consensus, perhaps the views of yo
nds. You will know what's right. Your life; your choice. I
y to make mistakes from time to time, so long as you lea
them. Don't hold grudges. Don't expect anyone else to
fect. By now, your mum and dad will have set your mor
pass and you will know right from wrong. The rest is up
. Have a good life, Sebastian. Do the right thing. I aske
do you know what the right thing is?' His answer w
futable. 'That's the point. You always know what the rig

17 October 2008

Dear Sebastian,

My father died of cancer when I was 14. It was a very hard blow for me and my family. Being young, I didn't fully appreciate – or value – how precious and fragile life is.

Now, looking back, I understand that the time I spent with my dad, especially those quiet, seemingly ordinary moments when we were alone, was very important, something to treasure for the rest of my life.

I know that, for you, the 9 years you spent with your dad will be time for you to look back on with fondness. For the early years between father and son are the most important, uncomplicated and valuable.

Losing a parent when you are young hurts badly but does impart one very important lesson about living that I quickly understood: never take the gift of life for granted. Your life and your health are precious gifts and that applies not just to you but those you love and care for.

From that simple precept, a number of virtues logically flow. One of those, which my father reminded me of shortly before he died, was the importance of being sensitive to the feelings of others, those you work with, your neighbours and friends.

The widow who has lost her husband, the family who have fallen on hard times, those around you who have met misfortune of one kind or another.
Don't turn away if you can help in any way.

When you are older, with your formal education behind you, try to choose a career doing something you have a passion for, which is not necessarily the calling that will make the most money but the work that will give you the most satisfaction.

Horses are my passion, always were, long before I discovered that I could make my living in my chosen field. So I would say to you, Sebastian, follow your passion in your chosen walk of life. If you love what you do, you can't wait to get out of bed in the morning to get started.

You will work longer and much harder if you love what you do. For example, a man with a small corner shop who stays open 18 hours a day, or a farmer with machinery who will work happily from dawn to last light. If you enjoy what you do, it is not a chore. And to go back to the beginning of this letter, if you value the gift of life and understand how precious it is, you might conclude that we are lucky to be here and blessed with the capacity to work hard. Maybe those of us who lose our dads have to work that little bit harder and that is no bad thing.

Never forget, Sebastian, that from time to time life tests us all. We endure misfortune, we make mistakes, sometimes we think we know it all, other times we wonder if we know anything. We are, in other words, human. Nobody knows it all, everybody fails in one way or another. Always keep some perspective.

Whenever you feel sorry for yourself, look around and you will see many who are less fortunate than you.

No matter whether you succeed or fail in your chosen profession, the quality of your life will be determined by the way you treat those closest to you, your family and friends. In business, never be afraid to ask questions if you don't understand something. Even when something is explained to you and you still don't 'get it' and feel foolish for asking again ... ask the question.

I never understood the dot.com bubble and was too proud to ask anyone to explain it to me. An expensive mistake *you* shouldn't make. If you are with interesting or successful people ask them lots of questions and don't say much yourself. It's important to listen, often more important than talking. When God created you, he gave you 1 mouth and 2 ears. Therefore, listen twice as much as you talk!

In a more personal sense, if you have nothing good to say about someone, say nothing. If you have an argument with a member of your family, sort it out before you go to sleep.

Never forget that whether in business or in personal matters, what goes around comes around. Look after those who love you, they are very special people.

With my very best wishes,

John Magnier

John Magnier

John Magnier is Ireland's leading thoroughbred stud owner. His stable, Coolmore Stud in County Tipperary, is the world's pre-eminent stallion nursery. He served as a senator in Seanad Éireann between 1987 and 1989.

Independent News & Media PLC

Group Headquarters
Independent House
2023 Bianconi Avenue
Citywest Business Campus
Naas Road
Dublin 24

25 August 2008

My dear Sebastian,

A famous American writer, John Gunther, wrote a memorable book called *Death Be Not Proud* about an event of a similar nature in his life.

Your father's courage adds lustre to these words and will be a symbol to you of all that is good and wonderful in your life ahead.

Sir Anthony O'Reilly
Chief Executive

Sir Anthony O'Reilly

Sir Anthony O'Reilly is a former rugby player and one of Ireland's most successful businessmen. Between 1955 and 1970, he won 29 caps for Ireland and also completed 2 tours with the British and Irish Lions. He went on to have a successful career with Heinz, becoming the company's chairman in 1987. Since leaving Heinz in 1998, he has pursued a variety of business interests.

From: Louis Copeland

To: Christine Horgan

Sent: 10 September 2008 11:43

Subject: Dear Sebastian

Dear Sebastian,

I suppose the most important lesson that life has taught me is that although my business has played a huge part of my life, it has really always only been a means to an end. That end has always been to provide the best possible life for those people whom I surround myself with on a daily basis – i.e. my family.

I didn't finish school as a child – I went to work in my father's shop from the age of 13. I suppose one of my biggest regrets (thankfully I don't have many!) is that I didn't educate myself further. It didn't seem that important to me at the time, and I suppose I will never know for definite if it hindered me, but, to this day, I fully believe that every day you wake up, you learn something new.

Always keep an open mind – you will never know it all, and sometimes the best ideas come from the most surprising of sources.

I strive every day for perfection in my business – but money is not my motivation. I want anybody who needs to buy a suit to know that Louis Copeland's will give them the best quality suit that their money can get them. I want the man wearing my garments to feel good about himself when he wears them. I want the man to be satisfied that Louis Copeland's gave him the best services, the best advice and the best value that this hard-earned money entitled him to have.

I suppose like everyone else out there, I'd be lying to say there's not a part of all this that does feed my ego ... But ...

Most of all, I want my family to know that everything I did during my time was an effort to make them proud.

Our business motto may well be 'The Customer is King', but the real Kings, Queens, Princes and Princesses are the ones I go home to every night.

I wish you every success and happiness.

Louis

Louis Copeland

Louis Copeland is a master tailor and menswear retailer whose grandfather established the family business in the early 20th century. The company has 4 outlets in Dublin and its many celebrity clients include Bono, Bill Clinton, Tom Jones and Pierce Brosnan.

NCB Group Limited
3 George's Dock
IFSC
Dublin 1

11 September 2008

Dear Sebastian,

Your father asked me to write to you with my thoughts and advice on how to live a happy and fulfilled life.

I know you must be missing your father very much and feeling very lonely and disappointed that he is no longer with you. My own father died when I was quite young, but not as young as you are now, so I understand your feeling of great sadness. Remember that your father will be watching over you and that you have a wonderful mum, grandparents, family and friends, all of whom love you very much.

My first piece of advice would be to put all your enthusiasm and commitment into everything you do, whether with family, friends or others and whether at school, sport, leisure or, subsequently, at work. You will find that life will be more enjoyable both for you and for others. You will also have more fun and will laugh more as will those around you.

Treat people with respect and fairness at all times, not only your family and friends but those in authority and those with whom you will come into contact when your working life begins. You will achieve far more and be a much a happier person by doing this rather than shouting, or screaming, or adopting a bullying approach. It will make your dealing with others more enjoyable and worthwhile both for you and for them, and you will get a greater enjoyment from life.

Be open and honest both with yourself and with others. Think straight, talk straight and be truthful at all times and you will never regret it.

Enjoy school and the learning experience. Try to discover the subjects or areas you enjoy most and find the most interesting. These may be academic subjects, trade or craft-related activities or other creative endeavours. Which of these areas do you most enjoy? Could you imagine yourself working in these areas in your future career? At your age, I had no idea what I wanted to do when I left school and I am sure you are the same. However, over the years, I gradually came to realise that I was interested in business and financial matters but had little aptitude for science subjects or technical areas. You will also discover, over your school years, those areas in which you are really interested. You may very well display your father's creative talents and go on to start up your own business.

Having decided what interests or excites you most, try your very best to obtain a qualification or trade or skill in this area. This will permit you to work at something you enjoy and are good at and should provide you with an enjoyable, worthwhile and fulfiling career for your working life. It will also mean that should you wish to travel and work abroad, you will be welcomed as someone bringing valuable skills to your new environment. My work as an accountant involved extensive travel overseas for a number of years. It was a source of great joy to me that I had the educational skills to do this and could have made a career as an accountant in any of these countries. Your father had an extremely successful career and worked in Australia and other places abroad. You may choose to do the same and a qualification or trade or skill will help you to achieve this.

Like so many people of my generation, I ended up working far too hard, to the detriment of family, friends and other areas. Do not make this mistake. Work hard but remember there are other things in life. Laugh a lot, relax and enjoy every moment.

Remember, again, that your late father will be watching over you. It was a source of great pride to me that I followed my father into accountancy, although he had died before I had passed my chartered accountancy exams.

Make sure that your father would be proud of you in everything you do and pray for him frequently.

Yours sincerely,

Breffni J. Byrne
Chairman

Breffni Byrne

Breffni Byrne is chairman of NCB Stockbrokers and a non-executive director of a number of companies including Irish Life & Permanent plc, CPL Resources plc, Hikma Pharmaceuticals plc, Coillte Teoranta and Tedcastle Holdings. A chartered accountant, he was formerly a senior partner of Arthur Andersen in Ireland.

4 September 2008

My dear Sebastian,

I have been asked to write to you to try and give you some words of advice. This follows the tragic death of your father at too young an age.

I have a number of basic principles which I have stuck to all my life. The first is: if you give loyalty, you will receive it; be discreet; have trust and that enables trust to form. Nearly all of my friendships are of many, many decades and I value them very much indeed.

With regard to my work ethic, I have a strong belief in myself and, above all, have the maxim never to give up. No matter how many times one fails, keep on trying. A famous oil man called Marvin Davis sunk 164 dry wells before he struck oil and I am sure that he was tempted to give up many times. You must also have self-belief, self-confidence and you must try to motivate yourself, others cannot do it for you.

If you are successful in life, and I hope you are, then remember to give something back to your fellow man and/or do something for your country. I call my national service, if you will, when I served as chairman of Telecom Éireann for 13 years and chairman of the Racing Board for 5 years for which I did not take personal remuneration.

I hope the foregoing is of some value to you in your life and I wish you every success. I send you my best regards.

Yours very sincerely,

Dr Michael Smurfit

Dr Michael Smurfit

Dr Michael Smurfit is a businessman and philanthropist. He retired as chairman and CEO of Jefferson Smurfit Group but oversaw the company's 2005 merger to create the Smurfit Kappa Group. The postgraduate business school of UCD is named after him because of the support he offers the school. He is a former director of AIB Bank plc and the former chairman of Telecom Éireann and the Irish Racing Board.

COLM ALLEN
SENIOR COUNSEL

Dear Sebastian,

You and I have never met.

What has established a connection between us is the remarkable man who was your dad, Jordan Ferguson. Sadly, he is no longer alive but he is still very much in your life and his legacy to you is one of which you can be truly proud. Follow his example and I don't think you will ever go too far wrong in life.

When your grandmother, honouring your dad's commitment to *Dear Sebastian*, wrote to me asking that I contribute to the book my first reaction was – Why on earth would Sebastian Ferguson want to hear from an ageing lawyer like me? Having wrestled with this dilemma it came to me that your dad would not approve of such negative thinking.

So here goes!

A very senior colleague of mine at the Bar (now long dead) gave me what I believe to have been very sound advice. He was talking to me about envy and the green-eyed monster. He made me see that being jealous of someone else, for whatever reason, is such an empty and corrosive emotion and touches no one but he or she who is troubled by that toxic way of thinking.

My own dad, whom I loved very much and still miss 8 years after his death at the ripe old age of 85, taught me 2 great lessons in life:

1. Never take anyone or anything for granted. Your dad could not have expected that his time on earth would be cut so short, yet it happened. Enjoy every day of your life to the full.

This is the second piece of advice which was fundamental to his philosophy of life:

2. *Carpe diem* – seize the day! When you find yourself in a good place or having a wonderful time, stop and savour it. Ask yourself, How good is this? How lucky am I?

Sebastian, there is so much more I could say to you but I was invited to write a letter not a book!

One last thing, hold fast to your mum and your grandma, and your other family and friends. Honour them and cherish them even when at times you may think they are barking mad or embarrassing or both.

I look forward to meeting you and celebrating when *Dear Sebastian* is launched.

Take care of yourself and those around you.

Every good wish,

Colm Allen

Colm Allen

Dubliner Colm Allen is a prominent practitioner at the Irish Bar. He became a senior counsel in 1992 and is a member of the Bar of England and Wales. He is chairman of the Rehab Group, which is the largest not for profit organisation in Ireland employing 3,500 people in 6 countries. Married to Amanda, he has 2 sons, David and Ben.

l'Ecrivain Restaurant
109a Lower Baggot Street
Dublin 2

10 September 2008

Dear Sebastian,

I am writing to you as a father of an 18-year-old daughter and a 12-year-old son myself. I cannot imagine having to do and cope the way your brave dad, Jordan, did.

My best advice is: be true to yourself. Be realistic when setting your goals. Remember goals are dreams that you make happen. Your father has left you a rich legacy from his short but very productive life. He will always be with you.

Also, remember your family. They have had a huge loss, too. You should discuss all your hopes and dreams with your family and keep them in your life. They miss your dad very much also.

Never be afraid to cry. Never be afraid. Be proud of who you are. Life is for living. Those who have left this life before us, especially your dad, have left it a better place for being here – never forget that. Never forget that he left you with all the hopes and dreams you could wish for. The world is your oyster – go out there and find the pearls. Good Luck!

With every good wish for your future.
Yours sincerely,

Derry Clarke

Derry Clarke

Derry Clarke is a chef who opened Dublin's l'Ecrivain restaurant in 1989. His ethos of keeping food simple has won many awards for his restaurant, including an Evian Michelin Star.

MARTINSTOWN
STUD

15 September 2008

Dear Sebastian,

I enclose some thoughts for inclusion in the *Dear Sebastian* book, which I hope you feel are suitable.

1. When you get up in the morning and things are looking bad, by the time that night comes, you only wish it was morning again.

2. When going through a bad patch, I often think of this old saying – It won't always be dark at 5 o'clock.

3. If you're lucky enough to swim the channel once, there's nothing to be proved by swimming it back.

The following TV ads always struck a chord with me.
'You never get a second chance to make a first impression.'
'It's the fish John West reject that makes John West the best.'

Best wishes,

J.P. McManus

J.P. McManus

J.P. McManus is a businessman and racehorse owner. He owns one of the largest number of horses in National Hunt racing and has many other interests including the GAA and golf.

Dear Sebastian,

You have been dealt a horrible blow so early in your life. The death of a parent is always a huge moment for anyone. To lose your father when so young is especially hard to bear.

You will remember your father as a young man who loved you dearly, and whose deepest regret was not being around to watch you grow up and advise you in the ways of the world. I have 2 teenage boys myself and that's exactly how I would have felt if I had been in your father's position. Treasure the memory of his love and his bravery. It's a wonderful starting point and foundation stone for you.

Life can disappoint us all. Friends, and even family, fall short of our hopes and expectations from time to time. It is so important, however, to remain optimistic about human nature. Expect the best from people, but prepare yourself not to be devastated when you do not meet it. Even though this is hard advice to follow sometimes, you will be well rewarded if you do. Trust given is usually returned. If you let down others, you will be more easily forgiven if they have received the benefit of the doubt from you.

I know, Sebastian, you are going to have to work all this out for yourself in time. I have found it enormously helpful to expect the best while trying not to be taken by surprise when one meets much less.

Like you, I was not born in Kinsale. I have lived most of my life there though. It is a wonderful place to live or to visit. Take advantage of it.

Warm regards,

Conor Doyle.

Conor Doyle

Conor Doyle

Conor Doyle is a Cork businessman and barrister. He is the director of the Doyle Group and chairman of the National Sculpture Factory. He is also the former president of Cork Chamber of Commerce and the former chairman of Cork Harbour Commissioners. Conor has raced yachts for more than 30 years and has been crowned Irish and European Dragon (30-foot class) champion.

International Investment and Underwriting
IFSC House
Custom House Quay
Dublin 1

2 September 2008

Dear Sebastian,

None of these letters will be more precious to you than your dad's would have been.

I don't think I am the best person to offer advice, as I am the last person to take it! I like to take risks and do things differently and, for the most part, I have been lucky. I am a good listener but have little or no patience and break all the rules! However, if I do have any words of wisdom to offer it would be that kindness is more important than wisdom.

I enjoy reading, remembering and citing quotes that I come across and have used this Ralph Waldo Emerson one repeatedly (when I used to give speeches). It particularly appeals to me because we can all relate to it, with or without ability.

'To laugh often and much; to win the respect of intelligent people and the affection of children; to earn the appreciation of honest critics and endure the betrayal of false friends; to appreciate beauty; to find the best in others; to leave the world a bit better whether by a child, a garden patch, or a redeemed social condition; to know even one life has breathed easier because you lived; this is to have succeeded.'

We must all recognise that we are only passing through and that life is only on loan. Our maker, in his infinite wisdom, determines the length of our stay. We should never forget or doubt his infinite goodness.

Never forget your dad succeeded because you are his son.

May I wish you a long and happy life with lots of fun along the way.

Yours sincerely,

Dermot F. Desmond

Dermot F. Desmond

Born in Cork, Dermot F. Desmond has founded and been involved in many high-profile business ventures, including NCB, Baltimore Technologies, Esat Digifone, London City Airport & Vivas Healthcare, as well as making a substantial number of investments in a variety of businesses worldwide, most notably Sandy Lane Hotel (Barbados), Celtic Football Club, Rietumu Bank (Latvia), Betdaq, Chronicle Bookmakers, The Sporting Emporium, Daon & Titanic Quarter (Belfast). He is also chairman of Respect, a charity set up by the Daughters of Charity to help develop their services to people with mental and physical handicaps.

Quinn Group
Derrylin
County Fermanagh
Northern Ireland
BT92 9AU

29 September 2008

Dear Sebastian,

It was with great sadness that I learned of the untimely
death of your dear father, Jordan, earlier this year. No doubt
you miss him every day. From what I have learned about
him, he was a courageous and exemplary father who had
tremendous pride in you and wanted to ensure you had the
best opportunities in your future life.

My own father died in 1967 when I was 21; that was
6 years before I started the Quinn Group. Times were very
different in 1967 in Ireland and my mother, along with my
sisters and brother, were devastated. With very little
means of income, we all had to grow up quickly.
While it does not compare to your loss at such a young
age, I think it also shows that a lot of changes are possible
in a short time.

From my father, I learned the value of hard work and
determination and, in many ways, the success of our
company is due to these same attributes which I have tried
to ensure were adopted by the Quinn Group over the years.
Many times in making important decisions about the group,
I would find myself considering what he would have done
and how he would have approached different problems.

Can I wish you every success in the future, Sebastian, and
while you will no doubt find your own path in life, remember

also that the example that your father has already given you will be your guidance in the most unexpected ways in the years ahead.

Good luck and take care.

Yours sincerely,

Sean Quinn
Managing Director

Sean Quinn

An astute business man and one of Ireland's best known entrepreneurs, Sean founded the Quinn Group in 1973 of which he is now group chairman and managing director. He successfully transformed a small family quarry business into a significant privately owned group employing over 8,000 people. Over the past 35 years the Quinn Group has developed into a multinational organisation with diverse business interests throughout Europe and Asia, and has successfully branched into new market sectors including: cement and concrete products; container glass; financial services; renewable energy and waste disposal; hospitality; radiators; plastics; packaging and property.

Dear Sebastian,

When I was growing up, my dad was a hero to me, and I wanted to be like him. In fact, I went through a short period when I idolised him and copied some of his mannerisms.

When my dad noticed this, he said to me, 'I don't want you to grow up to be like me, son, I want you to grow up and be like yourself.'

The wisdom of his words, and the honesty of them, stick with me to this day.

Kind Regards,

Brody Sweeney

Brody Sweeney

Brody Sweeney

Brody Sweeney is an entrepreneur who in 1988 founded, and is CEO of, O'Brien's Sandwich Bars. He is also on the board of Paddy Power and is a public speaker and author. In 2005, he co-founded Connect Ethiopia, a charitable foundation creating links between Irish and Ethiopian businesses.

12 October 2008

Hi Sebastian,

We have never met, I hope we do meet sometime. I know you spend a lot of time in Kinsale, with your granny. I have never been to Kinsale. I am told that it is a very beautiful and colourful town beside the sea. I was born in Spiddal in the Connemara Gaeltacht, my home town is also beside the sea.

When I was your age, I picked periwinkles and sold them on the market in Galway city. This paid for my first bike. The experience also provided me with one of the best lessons I have ever learned. Periwinkles can be found under rocks on the sea shore and, quite often, one has to turn over a number of rocks before you find the winkles. Just like life, sometimes you have to look in a number of places before you find what you are looking for, but never give up – keep turning over the rocks.

Do you ever go down to the sea shore, look out across the waves and wonder how nature is so powerful and, yet, so peaceful and beautiful?

Next time you take a walk by the sea let your mind float on the tide. Where does it bring you? What do you think of? Who do you think of?

Imagine what land lies on the other side of this sea: Who lives there? What language do they speak? Do they play football and hurling or have they some other sport? They have families and friends just like you and me. Some day, you will go across the sea to those lands. You will meet the people there, you will eat their food and you will learn about their lives. You may even learn their language and customs.

You will make new friends, some who come from far away places, and they will become part of who you will become as you grow into a young man. Choose good friends, people who will be with you whenever you need them. Good friends become anchors when the sea gets rough and turbulent.

We have seen what happens to the sea when a gale blows. If we have good friends, we will not be tossed all over the place because real friends help us weather those storms.

The best anchors are your family, they will always be there for you, and you will be there for them. They will cuddle you when you are down, they will help direct and guide you on the way up and they will celebrate your successes when you get there.

Like everything, you have to work on family and friends, do whatever you can to help them, be a team player. Create strong relationships based on integrity. Always be on the lookout as to how you can help people, while respecting their uniqueness. We are all dependent on each other. The unique power of people is truly amazing. Every person on this earth is as important and special as everyone else.

As you walk along the sea shore, think of people who mean most to you. What can you do to make them proud of you? What inspiration can you get from them?

What do you want to achieve in the next month, in next 6 months? It may be a certain result in school exams, become a better friend to someone, get on the school football team. Just make a quiet promise to yourself that you will do your best to achieve the goals you set for yourself.

Also, there is one very important thing to remember; all you can do is your best. You will not achieve every goal you set yourself, do not let that get you down. Do your best with integrity and help as many people as you can on the way. It is all about the journey, not the destination.

Never be afraid to try something new or different, especially don't be afraid to fail. After all, we are only human.

In years to come, you will travel far from this shore and experience new and exciting lands and people. But you will always come back to your roots, to where you came from and, as you walk the shore again, you will compare the world with you to the world without you.

Let's walk that seashore together
sometime.

Dia leat,

Padraig Ó Ceidigh

Aer Arann

Padraig Ó Ceidigh

In 1994, Padraig Ó Ceidigh purchased Aer Arann, the airline that from
2002 to 2005 was voted the fastest growing regional airline in Europe.
In 2002, he won the Entrepreneur of the Year Award and, in 2003,
represented Ireland in the world finals in Monte Carlo. He was invited
to be a world judge in 2004 and 2005, the first Irish person to be a world
judge for 2 years running. An alumnus of Harvard Business School, in
2005 he was honoured with the National University of Ireland, Galway
(NUIG) alumni business award and is also adjunct professor in NUIG.

Head Office
Bank of Ireland Group
Lower Baggot Street
Dublin 2

9 June 2008

Dear Sebastian,

Your father asked me to write to offer a suggestion on life in
the tragic circumstances that you will lose your father in the
midst of your childhood.

As a lifelong sailor, I was invited to lead the Irish Olympic
Sailing Group some years ago. This group was charged with
developing Irish sailors for participation in the Olympics. My
involvement was at the time of transition from amateurism
to professional sailing, and so resources for training, coaching,
foreign competition and equipment were scarce.

Some sailors coped better than others. Some complained
endlessly about lack of resources but others took maximum
advantage of what was available.

These differing reactions were a challenge to manage,
especially as some of those who moaned loudest had the
best natural talent. And then, one day, I went as a guest to
an Australian Rules football game in Adelaide, South
Australia. The local team – the Crows – won, after a tense
and fairly brutal battle.

After the match, some other guests and I met the coach to
the Crows. And, over dinner, he talked about his philosophy
about getting the best out of his players. He talked about
imbuing players with a sense of personal responsibility for
what they did; a need to appreciate the support systems

around a team but not to expect that the support would do everything.

He summarised all this in a phrase consisting of 10 two-letter words, 'If it is to be, it is up to me.'

This summed up for me the personal responsibility we all have to get on with life, whether you are an Olympic sailor or an artist, a team player or a solo player.

As you look forward to your teenage years and, beyond, to manhood remember the 10 by two. Accept all the help and support you will receive but do not be afraid to be your own man.

Good luck to you on the voyage of life,

Yours Sincerely,

Richard Burrows

Richard Burrows

Richard Burrows is a sailor and lifelong sports supporter. He was governor of the Bank of Ireland, president of IBEC, and co-chief executive of Pernod Ricard. Today, he serves on the boards of Carlsberg, Rentokil Initial and Mey Ichi.

 **Thomas Crosbie Holdings** Limited

15 October 2008

Dear Sebastian,

You have a great Dad. Just because someone isn't 'around' all the time does not mean they are not 'there'. It doesn't matter how long you spend on this earth, it's what you do while you're here that counts. In his 35 years, your dad did more than most people do in twice that time. I didn't know him, I'm sorry to say, but from what I have heard, he sounds like a pretty good role model to follow.

So my advice, Sebastian, is: as you go through your life (starting now), when you are faced with difficult decisions ask yourself, 'What would Dad have done?'

You will have a great life because you have great genes.

Good luck,

Alan Crosbie

Alan Crosbie

Alan Crosbie is the 5th generation of his family to run Thomas Crosbie Holdings Limited, the parent company of Examiner Publications, of which he is chairman. He is a former president of the European Newspapers Association, the director of the Press Association (London), chairman of the Press Association (Ireland) and, in 2006, was appointed adjunct professor of the John C. Kelleher Family Business Centre in UCC. In September 2002, he became president of Down Syndrome Ireland.

Dear Sebastian,

I have just been lucky enough to hear your dad on the radio. It's a sunny Thursday in June 2008. I'm living and working within a couple of miles of Jordan here in Kinsale. I made this choice for a set of reasons, the most important of which involved my father.

In July 1980, I left school for a year of travel and duly hopped on a ship sailing out of the famous port of Southampton heading to Australia via all sorts of fantastic places – new sights, smells, people, ship-mates from all over the world. After months of wandering, I was working on a cattle station in the Northern Territory of Australia, tens of thousands of acres, freedom and not a care in the world. One phone call changed my life for ever. Through the 10-second delay of radio telephone, my mother told me that a plane ticket awaited me at Darwin airport.

Twenty-four hours later, I was at Heathrow in a daze. Collected by my sister, we drove 2 hours, by strange coincidence, to Southampton, during which, they tried to explain that Dad was ill and in hospital. Sitting there in bed was a shadow of the man who had waved goodbye to me months before on the dock less than a mile from here. To say I was shocked is such an understatement, but, after a couple of days, Dad came home to rest and attempted to gain some strength.

It was July 1981, hot, sunny and glorious weather saw him resting under the shade of a large tree in our garden. Over the next few weeks of his life, I was able to sit and listen to him talk.

It soon became clear that this highly successful man had not enjoyed all aspects of his life. A 4-hour commute to the City of London for almost 30 years had taken its toll; perhaps it was this that induced the cancer. Having remained loyally with the same firm for most of those years, he had taken on a new and exciting job only days before his diagnosis. Should he have taken this type of chance years before? He came from a time of relative hardship. Growing up in wartime England and Ireland perhaps did not encourage one to take too many risks. Also a young family meant don't take risks.

These final weeks with him convinced me that, whatever you choose to do with your life, choose things you love. Do not compromise without certain knowledge that you will regret some of those compromises.

I came to live here when everyone else was going in the other direction because I knew this is where I should live, love and be satisfied with my life; thanks to him, I knew this to be the right choice. I said goodbye to my dad just before my 20th birthday. He was only 50 and I still think of him every day.

Anon.

as writing a lot of tiresome old waffle that might make m

great but would not be much good to you. Writing the le

made me realise something a bit humbling for a paren

no expert. My wife and I have three sons, all grown u

, decent generous, funny human beings. We are very prou

them but that's the way parents are. The truth is tha

y turned out well because of the decisions they made. Ye

y always knew they were loved, as you are, and they did n

e to worry about having a comfortable nest in which

, but they still had important decisions to make. You w

ide what kind of person you will be. A parent can hope an

urage, but the decision is yours. You will ultimately tak

credit, or the blame, for *Sport* n you will become, s

de now on some of your choices. Kind or cruel? Generou

ean? Honourable and honest or crooked and sleazy? A lor

e ago, on a fishing trip with a gentle, generous friend, w

e chatting after dinner and, in the way adults do after

ple of glasses of wine, I posed the philosophical question

at's it all about?' To my surprise, he didn't hesitat

at's easy. It's about doing the right thing.' Then, not f

first time in my life, I deployed my mouth without actua

ngaging my brain. I asked, 'How do you know what th

t thing is?' His answer was irrefutable. 'That's the poin

always know what the right thing is.' It's true, and if yo

t the simple, waffle-free philosophy to guide your life

t's it. The 'right thing' is not always the easiest or mos

venient thing, but you will know what it is, even when

s against the common consensus, perhaps the views of you

nds. You will know what's right. Your life; your choice. It

y to make mistakes from time to time, so long as you lear

n them. Don't hold grudges. Don't expect anyone else to b

ect. By now, your mum and dad will have set your mor

pass and you will know right from wrong. The rest is up

Have a good life, Sebastian. Do the right thing. I aske

v do you know what the right thing is?' His answer wa

futable. 'That's the point. You always know what the righ

Hi Sebastian,

My name is Seán Óg Ó hAilpín. I play sport as an amateur. I've been very fortunate to be part of Cork hurling teams since 1994 and I've been a member of the Cork senior hurling team for the past 13 years.

I live in Cork and have done for the past 20 years. I'm currently 31 years of age but life for me didn't start here in Cork. In fact, life for me started on the other side of the world. It's been a long journey to where I am today. I was born in 1977 on a tiny island in the Pacific Ocean.

The island is called Rotuma. It's where my mum is from. Look it up on the map but be very careful because you might miss it, it's that small! I lived on the island for 2 years and then moved to Sydney, Australia, where I spent the next 9 years. My father is Irish. He left Ireland to find work in Australia, went to Fiji on a holiday and met my mum. I'm the eldest of 6 children. I have 3 brothers and 2 sisters.

My years growing up in Sydney were fantastic – warm sunny days, playing sport with my friends till dusk, going to primary school in short pants and visiting a lot of my cousins who were living there also. To be honest, I couldn't have been any happier and thought my life was there for ever.

This all changed in 1987 when what usually would have been a routine day for me when I headed off to school that morning ended up changing my life for ever. When I came home from school, my mother broke the news that we were moving to Ireland. The thought of moving to a different place didn't sit well with me at all, especially when I had everything in Sydney. I knew my dad was Irish and he spoke about Ireland but I never really believed, in my heart of hearts, that Ireland existed. Or that we would move there.

I was proved wrong because we landed into Cork in February 1988. I arrived to Cork as a shattered and heartbroken 10 year old. I was devastated. Strange surroundings. Freezing cold and wet. No friends, no cousins and, more importantly, no rugby league which was the sport I played religiously in Sydney. In truth, I was afraid and I wasn't alone in that – my brothers and sisters felt the same.

Life in Cork for the next few years in my teens was tough, trying to get used to new surroundings. Trying to learn Irish at school was like pulling teeth and trying to grips with hurling was impossible. I had decided it was good for me to join the nearest sporting facility which happened to be the local GAA club as a way of making friends, introducing me to the community as well as keeping myself actively fit.

The biggest challenge I had to face was letting go of my Sydney days and the past. After 5 years of more downs and ups, I was resigned to the fact that Cork was my home. It's never easy trying to let go of something you love, but I had to if my life was to change. And by God, it did. For the better. My years growing up in Cork mirror the film *The Shawshank Redemption*.

If you haven't seen the film, I recommend you see it. It portrays an innocent man convicted for a crime he never committed. His first 5 years in jail were the toughest years he ever endured and all of this suddenly changed when he won the respect of the prison warden, prison guards and fellow prisoners. Like the film, my life changed full circle when I started excelling on the hurling fields at both club and school level. I began to earn respect from my team-mates, opposing players and, more importantly, from the local community.

In turn, my confidence and self-esteem rocketed to a new level. Great. I hadn't felt this great since my days in Sydney. Not alone did my hurling improve but my schoolwork started to improve also. I saw every marked improvement on the field of play and in my schoolbooks as an opportunity to work even harder and this pretty much kept me occupied to my late teens. I was so caught up with my commitment to sport and books that Sydney became a distant memory.

I now look back at that 11-year-old kid who arrived in Cork back in 1988 with pride. I still look at photos of the same kid around that time and all that I see is a frightened face and a broken heart. Twenty years on, I see a different face. I see a happy face and a heart as big as a lion to go with it. Are we born with happy faces and big hearts? No, we're not. If there's one thing life has taught me, it is that you make it happen yourself. You can only bring happiness and goodness to your life, no other person can. There's a saying, If it's going to be, it's up to me – and that's true.

When I arrived to Cork, I had 2 choices. I either had to make the most of my new life in Cork or sulk for the rest of it. I decided in the end to make the most of it. I admit that road wasn't easy to take. There was a lot of pain, hurt, tears, embarrassment, sacrifices and disappointments along the way but as Robert 'Bobby' Kennedy put it, 'only those who dare to fail greatly can achieve greatly'. I'm very grateful to my sport and school because they gave me a direction and commitment to that journey along the road. You know when you're on the right road when you get support from your family. I'm lucky to have amazing brothers and sisters and, without their support, I don't think I would have reached my destination.

Sebastian, what happened to you when you lost your dad was even worse than what happened to me when I lost my childhood. I know there's no day that you don't think of something you'd love to tell him about. I'm sure there are days when you think – just for a second – that you will get to tell him about it, and then you realise the truth.

I wish you the very best of luck on your journey. You remind me very much of the kid I was when I embarked on my journey. I know you'll reach the end of that journey with a happy smile and a heart as big as a lion because, if I could, you can. Expect sad days and setbacks, but create a life for yourself you'd be proud to tell your dad about.

Seán Óg

Seán Óg Ó hAilpín

Seán Óg Ó hAilpín is a hurling All-Star who captained Cork's senior team to the championship in 2005. He has won 3 All-Ireland senior medals and was a dual player, lining out for the senior Cork footballers. He is the only person to have been selected for both the International Rules and the Hurling/Shinty International Rules series.

From: Brian Cody

To: Christine Horgan

Sent: 29 September 2008 09:47

Subject: Dear Sebastian

Dear Sebastian,

I have had the pleasure for the past number of years of watching sports people living out the dreams they had as young lads. They had an ambition to achieve excellence in their chosen sport of hurling and seeing them achieve their potential has been a terrific experience.

It is for certain, Sebastian, that you, like all young lads, have ambitions, dreams, heroes and role models.

Have the confidence and self-belief to chase your dreams.
Have no regrets!

We get one opportunity – one chance at life. Make the best of it and make sure, while you're living your dream and reaching for the stars, that you keep both feet firmly on the ground and be a decent, genuine human being.

The very best,

Brian Cody

Manager, Kilkenny Senior Hurling Team

Brian Cody

Having completed a successful playing career with Kilkenny senior hurlers, which included 3 All-Ireland medals, Brian Cody has been the manager of his native county's senior hurling team since 1998. He has led the team to unprecedented success and is considered one of the greatest managers of the modern era. Under his management, Kilkenny has won 6 All-Ireland titles, including 3 in a row from 2006 to 2008.

Hi Sebastian,

I, too, lost my mother 'before her time', a shock, something that in any time of life fills us with immense sorrow. Of course, these tragedies happen to all of us at some stage in our lives and this is part of life.

It must now be 10 or 15 or maybe 20 years on, it is unimportant as I still I think about her like it was yesterday. She loved my brother and me as any mother loves her sons, unconditionally; she was always a presence in our lives that we thought of as timeless. What I realise now is that we never lost her, she is now more than ever with us,

I see her in the plants that grow, in the wind in the trees, in the smile of my son, in the birds that fly, in the sea I sail, in the voice of my brother, in the words of her friends, in the air we breathe and within my soul. And her constant presence more than ever guides us through life, in everything I do, I try to do well and hope that she is proud of us and what we do.

So I say to you ...

The love, the guidance, the presence and support of a loving parent stays with you always. Have a great life.

Damian Foxall

Damian Foxall

From Kerry, Damian Foxall is a professional sailor who has competed in 18 transatlantic races and 7 round-the-world events, logging over 310,000 nautical miles. He won the inaugural Barcelona World Race and has competed in the Americas Cup, the Volvo Ocean Race and the Olympics. In 2004, he was a member of the crew of *Cheyenne*, which set the Jules Verne record for the fastest circumnavigation of the globe in 58 days.

Dear Sebastian,

In my role as a rugby player early in my career, I was given some very sound advice and, as a result, my philosophy has been 'train as you play' – in other words, always give whatever you are doing 100% effort. Sport mirrors life: sometimes we win, sometimes we lose, sometimes it's not fair. If you can say to yourself 'I gave it my best shot', that's all anyone can do.

Very best wishes,

Brian O'Driscoll

Brian O'Driscoll

Brian O'Driscoll is a professional rugby player who plays centre for Leinster and Ireland. He has won 93 caps, 53 as captain. He led his country to the 2009 Grand Slam and, just weeks later, Leinster won their first Heineken Cup victory. He has scored 25 Heineken Cup tries, and was chosen as Player of the Tournament in the 2006, 2007 and 2009 RBS Six Nations Championships. In 2005, O'Driscoll captained the British and Irish Lions and, in 2009, embarked on his 3rd Lions tour.

12 November 2008

Dear Sebastian,

I am writing this letter to you in memory of your father, Jordan, whom I know you loved dearly and miss enormously. He was a man of great courage and dignity and I am sure the memories you have of him will last for ever. The picture I have seen of you on the beach together is incredibly heart-warming and brings a tear to my eye. Nothing can prepare you for such heartbreak.

You may not be aware that when I was 5 years old, and living in Lifford, County Donegal, I lost my mother to cancer and that's why I work actively here in Newcastle, and back home in Ireland, as the patron for Macmillan Cancer Support in the northeast of England. As such, I understand what you are experiencing.

In memory of your father, I am sure you will grow up to be just like he was before he was struck down with the illness – kind, considerate, loving and caring, and I'm certain that would have made him enormously proud.

Live your life to the full, keep your faith and grow up in memory of your father.

With very best wishes,

Shay Given

Shay Given

Shay Given is a goalkeeper from Lifford, County Donegal. He has played for Celtic, Sunderland (whilst on loan from Blackburn Rovers) and Newcastle United. He remained with Newcastle from 1997 until February 2009 when he transferred to Manchester City. He gained his first international cap in 1996 and is the country's most-capped goalkeeper with 96 caps to date.

25 September 2008

Dear Sebastian,

As you go through life, you will find that there is always something new to learn. You will also discover that there is little that is really new. Someone will always have done it before and will know how to do it. They will say, 'That's the secret.' In the old trades, the master craftsmen had what they called 'trade secrets'. These were skills that made their work special, a joy to behold. They jealously guarded these secrets and kept them to themselves, or at least within the family or the guild.

My earliest recollection is of trout and salmon and my granny, and it goes back to when I was about 2 years old. You see, I grew up beside a river, my father had a corn mill. In winter, I watched the adult fish riding the currents as they prepared to spawn. In summer, I saw the young fry in their thousands as they sheltered along the margins of the river. Sometimes, men would come, wearing rubber waders and coats smelling of beeswax and balsa, and fish and catch lovely golden trout on flies. I wanted to do that, too. I wanted to fly fish but no one would tell me how, and my father, who knew most things, didn't know either. It was a kind of 'trade secret' and these men were keeping it to themselves.

It has taken me more than 60 years to work it out and, while I am still learning, I would like to pass on these few tips to you, Sebastian, should you ever decide to take up fly fishing.

What is it that makes fly fishing so interesting? I think it is that when fly casting, the fishing is very much your own responsibility — and pleasure. You see the fish, make the cast, present the fly, hook it and land it all by yourself. Coupled with that is the joy you get out of fly casting. Using a spinning rod may be fun, but not pure enjoyment — fly fishing is.

Unfortunately, there are those who have fostered the myth that unless you were touched by the hand of God, you could probably never learn to cast a fly well. Nothing could be further from the truth.

Any normally co-ordinated person can learn to cast a fly with a few lessons from a competent teacher. Of course, you must practise as well. Fly casting is all about muscle memory and hand-eye co-ordination.

There are 3 stages in learning to fly fish.

1. Get a suitable, matched outfit — rod, line, leader and reel.

2. Learn to fly cast.

3. Spend the rest of your life fly fishing because there is always something new to learn.

When selecting a line, rod and reel, the wisest method is to have someone you know is competent to help you. Most people buy their fly fishing tackle in reverse order. They buy a rod, reel and line and some flies. That is wrong!

The first consideration should be the size of the flies that you will need for the kind of fishing you are going to specialise in.

Next, choose a fly line that will present them properly. It is important to understand how fly fishing tackle is matched, because it must be.

The first function of the fly line is to transport the fly to the fish. Fly lines are graduated according to a scale called the AFTMA scale, by weighing the first 30 feet of line. Its range is from # 1 to # 12. Basic guidelines suggest that you use a line to match the size of the fly – light lines for light flies and heavy lines for heavy flies. You would not haul a heavy piece of machinery on a pick-up truck and a light line is not capable of casting a heavy fly.

The second function of the fly line is to load the spring in the rod. Hence, the line must match the rod – neither too heavy nor too light.

The choice of fly rod is the next consideration and it must match the line. Every rod is matched to a specific weight of line, although most well-designed rods will cast a size heavier or lighter than the one that matches the rod perfectly.

The reel is the next consideration. For trout fishing, a simple well-made reel that will take the line and backing is sufficient. For salmon and saltwater fishing, the reel should allow the fish to take line against a smooth drag and then be retrieved under pressure.

The leader is the near-invisible connection between the fly line and the fly. Make sure it is properly designed. It should match the size of fly you are using and can be either hand-made or purchased. For dry fly fishing, always use a tapered leader.

We now come to the second stage in learning to fly fish — learning to cast a fly. I'd like to preface this section with the following remark: it's a great pity that fish can't read. Why do I say that? Well, if they could, I believe they would be mightily impressed by what they would read in the way fishing tackle is promoted. You know the kind of thing I mean: slick advertising, hefty prices and promises of what this or that piece of expensive equipment will do to improve your catches.

Always remember this. There is only one thing that impress fish — good presentation. The angler must be able to put the fly where the fish can see it. If he cannot do this, then it does not matter even if the flies are tied on golden hooks. You must learn to cast well, with ease and grace. Any normally co-ordinated person can learn to cast with a few lessons from a competent instructor. Find an APGAI – Ireland instructor in your area and take instruction. He or she will also advise you on the choice of fishing tackle, so don't buy any before you go. Afterwards, be sure to get in plenty of diligent practice.

There are 4 basic rules in fly casting which you should always remember.

1. Always begin a cast with enough line outside the tip of the rod to lead the rod and make sure that the line is straight. No squiggles!

2. The casting stroke is an accelerating stroke, followed by an abrupt stop. To help you with this, your instructor will teach you good rod-arm mechanics.

3. Move the rod top in a straight line. I call this painting the ceiling. Fly casting is all about controlling the loops of line. It is also about transmitting energy from the caster, through the rod, fly line and leader to the fly. Energy is transmitted most efficiently in straight lines. I repeat, learn to move the rod tip in a straight line.

4. Adjust the length of your casting stroke according to the length of line you are casting and the distance you wish to cast.

When the casting is not going well, refer back to these 4 rules and see which of them you are not following. The 3rd stage is learning to fish. This is the big one. You can choose your tackle in an afternoon. You can learn to fly cast with a few hours of good instruction. But learning to fish! This is a lifetime's pursuit. There is always something new to be learned about fly fishing, which is why we keep doing it from our youth to old age. If it were otherwise, we would learn it and then move on to do something else. But no. We continue to do it year after year. Fly fishing is very much your own responsibility – and pleasure. You make the decision and catch the fish all by yourself. Coupled with that is the joy you get out of fly casting. Using a spinning rod may be fun but fly casting is pure enjoyment.

My best advice on how to learn to fly fish is to find a friend – or a guide – who knows a little more about it than you, and have him take you along so that you can observe and learn.

You will learn, too, Sebastian, that there is more to fly fishing than catching fish. We live in an age of zoos and safari parks and 'out and take' fisheries. But we also need our wild places with clean water and clean air, and fish that are truly wild. Because there is no quiet place in our cities, we go to fish and listen to the rustle of the leaves, watch the flies dance above the bushes like angels in the clear evening air and the trout blow rings in the still pool. I know there are many who do not understand us anglers and this is not the place to explain. The shining water that babbles over the stones in the river is not just water. It is the blood of our ancestors. The lapping of the waves against the rocks on the lough shore as we drift by is the voices of our forefathers. The lively trout, darting back and forth in the stream, reminds you to make time for you children and have fun with them.

With all your strength, with all your mind, and with all your heart, preserve and protect the natural environment, both land and water, for your children and love it, as God loves us all.

Enjoy your fly fishing.

Yours sincerely,

Peter O'Reilly

Peter O'Reilly

Peter O'Reilly has been teaching fly casting for over 20 years and runs his own training school. He is the author of many books on fishing and the rivers and loughs of Ireland and is the chairman of APGAI – Ireland. He is also a fully qualified FFF (Federation of Fly Fishers) Master and THCI (Two Handed Casting Instructor). He has represented his country at international level at fly fishing and as a member of the Irish Clay Pigeon Shooting team.

From: Ronan O'Gara
To: Christine Horgan
Sent: 22 September 2008 13:15
Subject: Dear Sebastian

Dear Sebastian,

1. Play team sport if you can as it forms many great lifelong
    friendships. Also, the great victories and disappointments
    which you may experience make you able to deal with all the
    stuff that life throws at you (outside of sport).

2. You get out of life what you put into it.

Kindest regards and best wishes,

Ronan O'Gara

Ronan O'Gara
Ronan O'Gara is a professional rugby player who plays as fly-half for
Munster and Ireland, and who has toured 3 times with the British and
Irish Lions. He is the top points scorer in the 6 Nations Tournament and,
in March 2009, scored the drop-goal that secured Ireland's first Grand
Slam since 1948. In 2006, he was part of the Munster team that won
the European Cup for the first time.

Dear Sebastian,

My name is Pat Falvey and I am a
mountaineer, an explorer and an adventurer.
Like most people, I've had tough times, bad
times and good times in my life. It was hard
for you, at such a young age, to lose one
of your greatest mentors, your dad; it is in
light of a request from him that I write
to you now.

From an early age, my own father, along
with my mother and grandmother, encouraged
me to have dreams and to follow them. I
have been fortunate to be able to turn
many of these dreams into reality, and as
a mentor to you now, I ask you to look
into your heart, to have a dream and to
follow it.

Your dreams and ambitions will help you to
believe in yourself, to develop a 'go-for-it'
attitude and to trust in your own ability to
succeed. During your lifetime, you will have
many setbacks, of course, but if you can
treat these failures as a learning experience
and grow from them, then you will eventually

succeed, no matter what goals you set yourself.

My own dreams have been diverse and have changed at different times in my life. Turning these dreams into reality has taken me to the top of Mount Everest, to the freezing cold of Antarctica, to some of the most remote regions on planet earth, to deserts, glaciers and jungles. It has enabled me to meet some incredible people and to experience highs and lows, both in business and as an adventurer.

I have known the elation of success and the depression that we all experience when a venture fails or a dream dies. Most importantly, I have learned that life is wonderful and each day should be lived to the best of your ability. If you fall, pick yourself up; if something doesn't work, try again or start something new – above all, never give up.

When I was young, I got some sound advice that I have tried to build into my life. My grandmother, who couldn't read or write, but who was very wise said, 'If you think you can, you will. If you think you can't, you won't.'

Believe in yourself and in your abilities and you will succeed.

I left school at 15, and went into business. My only goal was to become a millionaire. I succeeded by age 21, and lost it all again by the time I reached 26. I lost confidence in myself and thought my life was finished. A good friend took me out mountain climbing. Our second climb was Corrán Tuathail, Ireland's highest mountain. That day, I realised it was, indeed, possible to overcome even the most difficult hurdles. There and then I set myself a new goal – that one day I would climb Mount Everest, the highest peak in the world.

Many said I was mad, that I couldn't do it. I believed I could. I did – and had a great time in the process. Now I've been to the top of the world twice (but I also failed twice!).

Never be afraid to dream big and never let a fear of failure stop you. One of my greatest mentors is my father, Tim, and one piece of advice he game me was to, 'Dream and dream big, but remember it's in the following of the dream where the success lies. Let achieving your dream be a bonus.'

To date, I have been on 64 expeditions. I have succeeded and failed both in business and on the mountains. I have had a great time following those dreams, and have achieved a number of firsts along the way, which has been a bonus.

Life can be a daunting challenge. Sometimes, we cannot succeed alone, but need the support of the team around us – those who love us, whose advice and care helps provide us with focus and determination, the people who help us to become the best we can be. The challenge of life itself can be compared to trying to climb the world's highest mountains. When you stand at the base of the mountain, you look up and wonder, How will I do this? The answer is simple – one step at a time.

Sebastian, I wish for you the wonderful life your dad wanted for you. I know he had many dreams for you. Now, you must find your own dreams and, remembering his advice, follow them through. I am leaving for Canada now, to plan for my next expedition, during which I hope to reach the North Pole. This will complete the Three

Pole Expedition – South Pole, North Pole and Mount Everest. Keep an eye out to see if I succeed.

Best regards,

Pat Falvey

Pat Falvey

Mountaineer, adventurer and motivational speaker, Pat Falvey led the first Irish team to trek to the South Pole and the first Irish team across the Greenland Ice Cap from east to west. He is the only person world-wide to have completed twice the Seven Summits Challenge (climbing the highest peak on every continent). He is the proprietor of Irish & Worldwide Adventures Training School.

Special Olympics
Europe / Eurasia

Providing individuals with intellectual disabilities opportunities for personal growth and community integration through sports.

1 September 2008

Dear Sebastian,

My name is Mary Davis and I work with Special Olympics which is an organisation that, through sport, changes the lives of people with an intellectual disability.

I love sport myself and have taken part in all kinds of sport activities from playing team sports to parachute jumping to running marathons, canoeing, skiing, climbing Kilimanjaro and Mont Blanc. I believe sport is a great way to learn other things in life. It helped me hugely to build my confidence, to experience success and failure, to work as a team, to travel and to meet all kinds of different and exciting people.

I work with Special Olympics because I know the value that people with an intellectual disability get from participating in the

Special Olympics programme. Last year, I attended the 2007 World Special Olympic Games in China with 210 athletes from all over Ireland. The thing that I remember most about those games in China was a big, huge poster that was plastered on every lamppost, billboard and public building. It was a picture of a smiling athlete and the words in Chinese and English 'I know I can' or in Chinese 'No xing, ni ye xing'.

The message in that picture rings loud and clear – the athlete is saying, 'Look at me – I'm capable, just give me a chance to show you what I can do!'

Special Olympic athletes have to overcome many obstacles and challenges in their lives but, over and over again, they have shown us how well they can perform, how brilliant their achievements are and what great fun they are to be with. It is their belief in themselves that gives me this belief in myself to go on and achieve in new areas that I thought may never be possible.

I have 4 children myself and my advice to them is always – I know I can!

Sebastian, enjoy your life, have some fun along the way and remember – you know you can!

Best wishes,

Yours sincerely,

Mary Davis

Mary Davis

Mary Davis was the CEO of Special Olympics Ireland from 1999 to 2008 and was the driving force behind bringing the Special Olympics World Games to Ireland in 2003. Through her work, she has dramatically changed the attitude of Irish society towards those with intellectual disabilities. She was the chairperson of the Taskforce on Active Citizenship and currently chairs the steering group established by the Taoiseach to implement the recommendations of the taskforce. She is managing director of Special Olympics Europe/Eurasia.

Molineux Stadium
Waterloo Road
Wolverhampton
WV1 4QR

Dear Sebastian,

I can only give you the same advice and guidelines
that I gave my own children and, indeed, the same that
was passed on to me by my parents. That is to be as good
as you possibly can at whatever you choose to do in life,
whether it's sport or your profession, etc. Just ensure
you do it to the best of your ability, try and do it with a
smile on your face, be polite, well mannered, good
natured, punctual and hard working. Overall, try to be
a good person.

We all try and live up to our parents' expectations and try
to make them proud. I think my children have got all the
qualities that I have previously mentioned and none of them
are high fliers in their jobs or in sport, but all 3 of them make
me extremely proud to be their dad, every single day.
If you can achieve that, then you can hold your head up
high and be proud of yourself.

Throughout your life, you will be given advice both
good and bad and it is what you make of it that will be the
difference. I was given some advice over 30 years ago by a
teacher who told me I wouldn't be good enough to play
football professionally and that I should get a proper job.
It is one piece of advice that inspired me to work even
harder to have a successful career in football.

I look back on this now and hope he said it with the intention of inspiring and motivating me to try harder and if that was his aim, then he certainly achieved it.

But it's one piece of advice I'm glad I didn't take!

Kind regards,

Mick McCarthy
Manager

Mick McCarthy

Mick McCarthy is a former soccer player and the current manager of Wolverhampton Wanderers FC. Born in Yorkshire, he played for several clubs including Manchester City and Celtic. In his international career, he won 57 caps and was part of the 1990 World Cup team before going on to manage the Irish team between 1996 and 2002.

Dear Sebastian,

As a young boy, my father and I would watch the World Snooker Championship on BBC TV every year, in awe. My father was an avid Ray Reardon fan; my favourite was Alex Higgins. When these 2 players contested the final in 1982, for us, as a sporting spectacle, it didn't get much better than this. My hero Alex won and thus became my inspiration to become a snooker player and professional. That same year, my father bought me a small snooker table for Christmas, which gave me endless hours of fun for many days.

My father passed away the following year and, unfortunately, only saw me play on that small table he purchased. He never got to see me play competitively and become World Champion in 1997. However, I always feel he's there watching from above. I realise now that he was my real hero, not Alex Higgins, he was my real inspiration along with my mother. They gave me the opportunity to realise my dream. They taught me the values of life and hard work. They taught me how to be the best I could be, without trying to be better than anyone else. They taught me the value of giving 100% and never giving up or throwing in the towel. They taught me the value of respect for others as well as myself, the value of love and friendship, honesty and morality. They taught me the value of sacrifice and hard work, that nothing comes easy, that goals achieved with little effort are seldom worthwhile.

All these things they passed on to me and I shall pass on to my own son and hope that he will listen and live by them.

I hope this can make some sense to you, Sebastian, and that your dad has passed on all the great values that he had learned during his life. I wish you well and good luck.

Yours sincerely,

Ken Doherty

Ken Doherty

Snooker player Ken Doherty turned professional in 1990, having won the World Amateur Championship a year earlier. In 1997, he won the World Professional Snooker Championship and became the only person to win both World Amateur and World Professional snooker championships. He is currently ranked 18th in the world. Ken is an avid Manchester United fan and is also well-known as a poker player.

Dear Sebastian,

Firstly, I would like to offer you my sincerest condolences. It is obvious that your father cared for you deeply. His desire that this project be completed is a testament to his love for you. I feel deeply honoured to be given the opportunity to participate in such a cause.

I don't know if I can offer you any wise words on how to live your life, but what I can do is tell you my own story. Hopefully it will help you in some way.

I retired from professional rugby on 31 December 2007, after playing for Munster for 10 years. When I finished college in 1997, I had earned a civil engineering degree and a post-grad diploma in computers, but still had no idea what I wanted to do in life. There was no direction, no obvious path for me to choose. In the weeks following my final exams, I spent more time watching daytime television shows like 'Countdown' and 'Neighbours' rather than considering my future options.

It was on one of the lazy afternoons spent on the couch that I got an interesting phone call. Jerry Holland, Munster's manager, was asking me to come to a meeting of about 40 players in Thomond Park. We were being introduced to Welshman John Bevan, Munster's new coach. Rugby had just turned professional and Munster were offering about 30 part-time contracts. I never for a second believed that I was going to be offered one of those contracts.

Rugby had never been a serious thing for me. I didn't go to Pres or Christians and I didn't have the traditional rugby pedigree. People within the establishment of my own club even stated that I would never be as good as a school's player. I was angered by these views but, unfortunately, I also half-believed that the doubters were right. So when I went to that meeting in Limerick, the self-doubt manifested itself and I laughed off any possibility of a career in rugby.

A few weeks later, John Bevan walked away from the Munster job. I don't think he was too impressed by the disparate bunch from the 6 counties and decided that a coaching role in Wales would be far more attractive. As a result, Munster were to be controlled by an unproven schools coach from Cork who had never played rugby beyond club level. He was given a 3-month contract and was there purely on a temporary basis. His name was Declan Kidney.

Not long after Declan's appointment, I, too, was offered a part-time contract. Ronan O'Gara and I were told to sign up after training one evening. There was no negotiation. On the corner of each of our contracts there was a number; 29 on Ronan's and 30 on mine. We were in by the skin of our teeth.

Even though I was in the squad, it never seemed a possibility to me that they would ever be crazy enough to select me. I was still shy of running beside Mick Galwey or Peter Clohessy during training. After all, up until a few weeks ago, they had been my rugby heroes. While I might not have believed in my own ability, Declan Kidney had certainly seen something he liked. Out of the blue one day, my name was called out in the list of players who would start against Cardiff in the European Cup. I was shocked. The night before the game, I could barely sleep with nervousness. But once the game kicked off, I was fine; I felt like I belonged. We didn't win that day but I performed well and scored a try. I also got a taste of European Cup rugby and decided that this was the career for me and that this opportunity wasn't going to pass.

I had 10 years in the professional game. There were moments of heartbreak and disillusionment. We lost 2 European Cup finals in front of our devastated supporters. There were years where no matter how well I was playing, an Irish cap seemed to be impossible. In these early years, the salary that was offered was barely enough to survive on. During these times, I relied on the willing support of my wife, Grace, and my parents, Maurice and Noreen. Then there were the goods times, like winning my first cap for Ireland and finally achieving the ultimate accolade of being part of the 2006 European Cup-winning side. I feel my wife and family contributed as much to that as I did and, without them, I wouldn't have been there. And these good times far out-weighed the bad.

I suppose these are some of the messages I'm trying to relate to you, Sebastian:

1.   Always believe in yourself and your own ability. Never let anyone tell you that you can't do something.

2.   Trust your family. They will always support you and guide you to doing the right thing.

3.   When you find something you are passionate about, go after it with as much effort as you can muster.

4.   And, finally, ride your luck! When things are going your way, take advantage of it.

I hope this story has been of some help to you and I wish you the very best for your future and I do believe that whatever path you choose, your father will be right there beside you.

Yours sincerely,

John Kelly

John Kelly

John Kelly became a professional rugby player for Munster and Ireland, playing on the wing, in 1997. He played in the 2003 World Cup and was a member of Munster's 2006 European Cup-winning side. He won 17 international caps and 153 Munster caps (he is the province's second most-capped player) before retiring from the game in December 2007.

<u>Christy O'Connor Jnr. Ltd.</u>
Golf Enterprises

Dear Sebastian,

Firstly, let me say how very brave you are. It is never easy to lose someone so close to you, and having experienced this awful tragedy in my own life, I know how very strong you must be.

This brings me to my first guideline: face this world with courage. Sometimes, when we are feeling that life has been unfair, have courage to believe in yourself and always remember that your dad will be looking over you.

During the early stages of my life, when times were tough, I always had belief in myself that, one day, my life would be better, and so I would always encourage you to believe in yourself and follow your dreams.

Of course, in order to achieve your dreams, you must be prepared to work hard. After many years of practising and practising my golf game until I could practise no more, I was successful in becoming a member of the PGA European Tour and later a member of all PGA tours, playing tournaments throughout the world. This was one of the biggest achievements in my life. However, always remember there will be many more challenges along the road and so continue to work towards every new direction your life takes as I did.

As life is not always about work remember to live life to the full as your own dad did. I would encourage you to travel the world and enjoy your life. I was very lucky that my own career enabled me to do this; there is so much to learn and experience.

Finally, for me, family and friends are so important, keep them close to you and always know that they are there for you no matter what.

It would be an honour for me to play a round of golf with you some day.

Yours sincerely,

Christy O'Connor Jnr

Christy O'Connor Junior

Irish golfing legend Christy O'Connor Jnr was at the forefront of the PGA European Tour for over two decades. His career to date has included 17 professional wins including four European Tour events, two Senior British Open titles, and two Champion Tour events. He has represented his country on over twenty occasions in the World Cup, the Alfred Dunhill Cup, the Double Diamond, the Hennessey Cup and the Ryder Cup. Christy is now actively involved in golf course design and his portfolio consists of over 30 golf courses worldwide.

Dear Sebastian,

Ever since I received your nan's letter, just a month ago, I have been thinking how to respond in a fitting way that would be meaningful to you and also as a fulfilment of your late great dad's wishes.

It's not easy to write such a letter to a young lad like you, Sebastian. But, today, I climbed Croagh Patrick for the first time. I was here in Westport with the Dublin and Galway teams that contested the All-Ireland in 1983 – 25 years ago, your dad would have been 9 years old then, the same age as you are now. I was thinking about you, your dad and your nan when up there on that sacred mountain, and I committed to writing this when I came back down.

When I, myself, was about 9 years old there was a hit song at the time, which went 'Do what you do, do well boy'. You know, it always stuck in my mind and I found in life when I had important things to do, that song came into my head and I just decided to do my best and let the rest take care of itself.

In life, you will be faced with loads of choices. You won't be able to do everything but follow the things that you are interested in yourself. Be prepared to try several things and hobbies and then keep those you like yourself. Remember, it's your life – make the most of it and the talents you have, but do it in a nice controlled way. Don't allow yourself to be too pressured by others and, especially when it comes to choices like drink and drugs, make your own mind up and don't be sucked into anything that you know, deep down, is not good for you and others. That will take courage but you will be a better man for it.

Hopefully, you will have a few close friends. One or 2 really good friends are all one needs while, at the same time, you can enjoy the company of a wider circle of friends.

Be proud of roots. I see you come from Kinsale – what a lovely town! One day, you might represent your club and county, might even be proud to see Cork beating Kerry. All that is good fun because if you are proud of your own place, you are proud of yourself and your family and that's the most important thing of all. And it's good to have dreams.

Life is meant to be enjoyed – not in a selfish way but in a way that everybody contributes to making life better for everyone else. They call that, sense of community and sense of place – big phrases for a 9 year old, but, in time, you will understand them.

Now, Sebastian, long letters can be painful. So I will finish up by wishing you a long and healthy life. Take care of your body, take care of your mind – eat well, sleep well and live well – and your late Dad, Jordan, and Nan and all your family and friends will be very proud. Do what you do, do well, and never worry about making a mistake.

Beir bua agus beannacht (ask your teacher what that means),

Sean Kelly

Sean Kelly

President of the GAA 2003–2006 and a proud Kerryman!!

Sean Kelly

By his own admission, Sean Kelly is a GAA man 'born and bred'. He has had close links with the organisation all his life and served as its president between 2003 and 2006, the first Kerryman to do so. Between 2006 and 2008, he was the executive chairman of the Irish Institute of Sport. He is currently a Fine Gael MEP for Ireland South.

Dear Sebastian,

The very fact that you are reading this letter means that life has already dealt you one of the cruellest blows of all, the premature departure of your father. I didn't know your dad and only got a brief insight to his character through his vision in compiling this collection of letters for you. You have much to be proud of.

Tragedy visits every household in some shape or form through the course of one's life. It is part and parcel of life itself. You have faced this experience earlier than most. When confronted with his illness, your dad dealt with it bravely and with honesty. That is a trait that will serve you well.

If I was to offer you any advice on how to live your life, all I would say is to be straight and honest in your dealings with people. Be what you are, be honest with yourself. Honesty generates respect. When you have people's respect, you don't need a whole lot more.

Have no regrets. Don't live your life wondering 'what if'. Of course, you will make mistakes along the way, everybody does. Learn and move on. Life is more fulfilling when you are part of something bigger than yourself. Team sport has taught me that. Just making a contribution is good enough. It may take time for you to find your niche. That is normal. Those who know exactly what they want to do with their lives at 18 years of age are few and far between. Talk to people. Don't be afraid to seek and take advice. I wish you well.

Donal Lenihan

Donal Lenihan

Donal Lenihan is a former Munster and Irish rugby player, who won 52 caps for his country and captained Ireland in the inaugural 1987 Rugby World Cup. He also played on 2 tours with the British and Irish Lions. After retiring from the game, he became the manager of Ireland from 1998 to 2000 and then took over the management of the Lions for the 2001 tour. He is an author, commentator and writes for the *Irish Examiner*.

From: Thomas Taaffe
To: Jordan Ferguson
Sent: 27 May 2008 09:55
Subject: Dear Sebastian

Dear Sebastian,

When I rode my first winner in July 1981 at the Phoenix Park, my father, a very quiet, humble man, who achieved all in sport, said to me the next day, 'It was great for you to ride your first winner but don't forget you are only as big today as you were yesterday' – and he walked away. I can still see him disappearing in the distance. The meaning: Don't forget where you came from and don't get carried away.

I have always remembered this and find it invaluable advice.

Otherwise, I believe 'work hard and play hard'. One must always try to take the positives out of life and the actions that happen therein.

Health and happiness,

Tom Taaffe

Tom Taaffe

Tom Taaffe is a National Hunt trainer based at Portree Stables in County Kildare. After retiring as a jockey in 1994, he has had success with many horses, including Kicking King, which won the Cheltenham Gold Cup in 2005 and the King George VI Chase in both 2004 and 2005; Finger On the Pulse, which won the Jewson Novice Handicap Chase at the 2008 Cheltenham Festival; and Ninetieth Minute, which won the Coral Cup at the 2009 Cheltenham Festival.

Dear Sebastian

I have always enjoyed writing letters. My generation of oldies never used the telephone much except for short conversations: neither mobiles nor computers were in existence. However, this is the hardest letter I have ever had to write.

Of course, the letter you really want to read should be from your dad. When he thought of this idea as a present for you, I urged him to write down his advice to you immediately. He said that if he wrote it, it would be admitting that he was about to die. He was so courageous, and optimistic that there was plenty of time – I could say no more and, as you know, he became very sick suddenly and then the time was gone.

I will, first of all, make the best guess I can about what he might have wished to pass on to you. On the back of an old envelope he had scribbled the words 'failures' and 'successes'. These words might have led to anything but I feel that he possibly would have told you never to be ashamed of your failures, but to learn from them, and never to boast about your successes.

One piece of advice I know he certainly would have given you (because he was always saying it) was never to be judgemental. That means never to think badly of others whatever they may say or do: you never know the reasons for their words or actions, and everyone sees situations from a different point of view.

The wisdom of that was really brought home to me some years ago. In 1993, Grandpa Ireland and I went on a holiday to Northern India with a group of people that we hadn't met before. At Delhi airport we were all reunited with our suitcases which were mostly small and compact, suitable for travelling in a country of people without many possessions. However, three people in a party together collected about seven large suitcases between them. I was horrified and whispered to Grandpa, 'Where on earth do they think they are going – they must have brought all their clothes with them from swimwear to full evening dress. Ridiculous!' At the end of our holiday, the three explained that they were staying on for a few extra days. They had come from a small village in England that had collected clothes, toys and medicines for an extremely poor community who lived up in the mountains. They had actually risked imprisonment by smuggling all the items in against Indian law, and were going to deliver them personally. Can you imagine how ashamed of my thoughts I felt? I never forget that lesson.

Don't judge yourself by others either. One of the last times that you were here in Kinsale with your dad, he was discussing school work with you. I was going to get some of his old school reports to show you. Yes, I do have them all and all his letters to me from boarding school too. He quickly stopped me from getting them because, as he said, you must never be put under any pressure to live up to anyone else. You must be proud to be your own person whatever you do in life. It isn't important whether you become a tycoon or choose to do a humble job and earn little money. Just 'go for it' and be the best you can. That is sufficient.

You have been given many varied pieces of advice from all the kind people who have written letters for this book. There isn't a thought in the letters which I would disagree with but there is an extra conviction of mine that I wish to share with you. It is something that my father, your great-grandfather, taught me. Wherever you are, observe the wonder of nature – the sea, the sky, the animals and the flowers. Remember when you were very young we used to turn over stones in my garden looking for the tiny insects. You built little, pretend houses for them with dining rooms, stairs and bedrooms! That showed me you have a very kind heart: never lose it. Even if, when you are grown-up, you live in a city, there are still birds in the sky, trees, flowers and *butterflies in the parks, and even the occasional determined weed peeping through cracks in the paving stones. (It is said that a weed is only a plant in the wrong place). There will always be the sun, moon and stars, although I know you will tell me that you can't see them every day. Try to see the beauty in all of creation. No matter how few possessions you may have, no one can take this away from you.*

I am quite sure that you already know how much your dad loved you. His last thoughts were about caring for you and compiling this book to help you through life without him. It is not easy, I know, but he wanted us all to be positive and to be happy.

Although most of our family live many miles apart, I am certain that we will always support you as best we can.

Remember, I will love you for ever.

Grandma Ireland
May 2009

Dad

Dad, he's amazing, he really is!
He's so young,
He can do anything, anywhere, anytime, anything,
It's incredible!
I don't know how he does it.

Dad, he's a mystery,
It seems out of this world,
Everything he does,
It seems ... AMAZING.
Maybe he's a robot! [Don't take it personally!]

Dad, he can take anything
He does everything so well
Swimming, art, sport, and every subject,
In every way he's perfect,
He is AMAZING!

LOVE,

SEB   XXXXXXXX

May 2008

Acknowledgements

My grateful thanks to Dr Tom Mullins for all his help and encouragement with this book and also to Simon Mooney for his invaluable assistance in researching many of the addresses of the contributors.

Clodagh Ross-Hamid, Gillian Maclean and many of Jordan's friends have shared with me the memories of his last days. I do appreciate this as I know that it must have been extremely difficult for them.

Maria O'Mahony (Finishing Services, Kinsale) and Aisling Ferriteur did all the administrative work – always with a willing smile. Thank you both for everything.

I am greatly indebted to my editor, Ciara Doorley, together with the team at Hachette Ireland and also my agent, Jonathan Williams. Their patience and sensitivity in guiding a novice 'author' has meant a great deal to me.

Of course, this book would not exist without the generosity of all the contributors. Many of them phoned or wrote personal letters of condolence to me as well as sharing their deepest thoughts with Sebastian. I will never forget their kindness.

I am also most appreciative of the financial help given to me by Betfair by funding my expenses during the inception of this book. Jordan worked with Betfair as Director of International Sales and Business Development for several years.

Finally, thank you to my husband, Pat, for all the love and understanding that he has given to me throughout the past year when so much of my time was spent working on this project.

Many medical agencies tended to Jordan, and helped me, during the last months of his life. I wish to acknowledge particularly St Vincent's Hospital, Sydney; the staff of the A&E department and St Therese's Oncology Unit, Mercy University Hospital, Cork; the Kinsale public health nurses; Collins Kinsale Pharmacy; Dr David Nagle's surgery; Arc Cancer Support House; and all the staff at Marymount Hospice, Cork. Their professionalism and compassion were simply outstanding.

Christine Horgan
July 2009

A contribution from the proceeds of this book have been donated to the Irish Hospice Foundation.